From Grief to Grace

D1565293

Jeannie Ewing

From Grief to Grace

The Journey from Tragedy to Triumph

SOPHIA INSTITUTE PRESS
Manchester, New Hampshire

Sophia Institute Press
Box 5284, Manchester, NH 03108
1-800-888-9344

www.SophiaInstitute.com

Sophia Institute Press® is a registered trademark of Sophia Institute.

Library of Congress Cataloging-in-Publication Data

Names: Ewing, Jeannie author.
Title: From grief to grace : the journey from tragedy to triumph / Jeannie
    Ewing.
Description: Manchester, New Hampshire : Sophia Institute Press, 2016.
    Includes bibliographical references.
Identifiers: LCCN 2016003964 ISBN 9781622822942 (pbk. : alk. paper)
Subjects: LCSH: Suffering—Religious aspects—Catholic Church. Loss
    (Psychology)—Religious aspects—Catholic Church. Grief—Religious
    aspects—Catholic Church.
Classification: LCC BX2373.S5 E95 2016 DDC 248.8/6—dc23 LC record
available at http://lccn.loc.gov/2016003964

First printing

*For all of the silent heroes and heroines
who carry their crosses without complaint
and embrace the joy that
every moment presents to them*

Contents

Appendices

Foreword

I have had the pleasure and honor of knowing Jeannie Ewing for eight years, and among her list of many accomplishments, she is a faithful and zealous Catholic, a great wife to her husband, Ben, a wonderful mother to her daughters, Felicity and Sarah, and a great friend. Jeannie and I met in the summer of 2006 as interns for the Catholic Campaign for Human Development. I knew then that I had met a very intelligent, determined, and passionate young woman. She is very involved in her home parish of St. John's in Goshen, Indiana, and an accomplished writer.

When Jeannie mentioned to me several months ago that she was working on a book on human suffering and the response of faith to one of the most difficult mysteries of God, I must admit that I thought it would be a difficult undertaking at the time, but I also knew that with prayer, careful reflection, and a deep faith, she would accomplish what she set her mind and heart to do. I have no doubt that, as you read this very heartfelt and thought-provoking book, you will be enamored with Jeannie's sincere and powerful story.

Even if you find that you cannot identify with every aspect of Jeannie's experience with suffering and the power of faith to overcome the obstacles that come from temptations to doubting

God and despair, I'm sure you will be able to come away with a few nuggets of insight that will help you accept your own sufferings as redemptive and transforming while you cultivate your own relationship with Jesus Christ.

After the births of Felicity and Sarah, I had the wonderful blessing of baptizing them. With the challenges on the horizon for both the children and their parents, the sacrament of Baptism became a moment of grace not only for the children but for Jeannie and Ben as they searched for signs that God was with them in their moment of sorrow and grief. You will find few parents more caring, compassionate, and resolute in their faith than Jeannie and Ben.

In my short time as an ordained priest (close to five years), I have had several opportunities to minister to people from all walks of life who have different opinions about faith, hope, love, and—above all—suffering. In particular, Jeannie points out rather candidly in this book the problem of suffering and how faith plays a role in overcoming many of the obstacles that suffering can present in our lives. Although she uses technical terms related to the field of psychology, which is her field of expertise, she writes plainly and succinctly to get to the heart of our deepest longings and purpose as human beings even when we are faced with the horrors of human suffering from time to time.

With examples from her own life and taking on some of the heavy topics debated in the public forum, Jeannie sets out on a course to discover what our Christian faith can do to combat many of the misconceptions, misunderstandings, and flat-out false notions that our society has presented to discount God's presence in all that we endure as human beings.

The tendency we often have is to doubt our ability to care for the most vulnerable, but our faith demands that we care for the least among us, as Jesus tells His disciples in the Gospels. How do we care for those in most need of our love and understanding even if at times we feel we just can't do it? Do we find ourselves asking at times: Where is God in this? Jeannie lays out beautifully a no-nonsense approach to how we might begin to answer these questions and to put into action the faith we have received from God.

Jeannie also relies on the great spiritual physicians of our Christian history—namely, St. John of the Cross and St. Thérèse of Lisieux—to help you discover that even the great saints of the Church struggled in their lives to make sense out of suffering and attempted to solve the puzzle that is the mystery of God's love. It is the examples of the lives of the saints, after all, that help us gain a deeper understanding of how we might grow closer to God through His Son, Jesus.

It is also through good spiritual direction that Jeannie was able to put into perspective the purpose that God was calling her and Ben to discover the unconditional acceptance of the children they were given. Sometimes we hear the world's voices telling us, perhaps in a very cold way, that these are "the cards we have been dealt" or that "God never gives you more than you can handle." While these serve as attempts to make sense of the suffering, grief, or even mourning we go through in life after some sort of loss, they are inadequate to penetrate the real reason God allows us to endure suffering at all.

Although Jeannie and Ben's daughters have some struggles and bumps in the road ahead, they are blessed to have parents who love them unreservedly, and perhaps through this love they will be able to share with the world how deep God's love is for all of us. His love is that bottomless well, the tunnel that goes on for miles and miles with seemingly no end in sight, or the cavern that is as deep as it is wide. Nothing suffices to capture the endlessness of God's love.

Jeannie has captured in this book the essence of human suffering and the answer to what may seem to be the *unanswerable* at times. The example she gives of her own life represents the true strength she possesses in knowing a God without bounds and in knowing how far we can go in this journey of faith, no matter what life throws at us.

In this book, Jeannie talks about mission that Jesus commissioned. He called the Apostles and disciples to go out into the world, not only to preach the Good News, the gospel, but to baptize in the name of the Father, and of the Son, and of the Holy Spirit. The word *commission* means "to be sent with a mission or with a purpose in mind." All of us have a purpose and a particular mission that God has given each of us so that we can use the gifts we have been given and share them with others who are in need of God's love and mercy.

To have the strength to carry out this mission, however, we need the Spirit of God, and so, when we are baptized, we receive this Spirit and die in Christ in order to receive new life. All life is precious, as we know, but to receive new life in Christ is especially precious, because no amount of money can buy it. Everything we do in life is meant for the purpose that God intends. This means that suffering, grief, disappointment, trials, and the internal struggles are part of the growth that strengthens our faith so that we can move mountains with our mustard-seed-size faith.

St. Paul tells us in his first letter to the Corinthians:

And no one can say, "Jesus is Lord," except by the holy Spirit. There are different kinds of spiritual gifts but the same Spirit; there are different forms of service but the same Lord; there are different workings but the same God who produces all of them in everyone. To each individual the manifestation of the Spirit is given for some benefit.... As a body is one though it has many parts, and all the parts of the body, though many, are one body, so also Christ. For in one Spirit we were all baptized into one body, whether Jews or Greeks, slaves or free persons, and we were all given to drink of one Spirit. (1 Cor. 12:3-7, 12-13)

It is this same Spirit who has inspired Jeannie to share her story. The fruit of this work is that it will inspire others to see the presence of miracles still at work in our world. Inherently we know that there are still miracles, but do we really believe that God can manifest His grace in us by showing us that no suffering, no trial, no struggle, and not even death itself can separate us from His love?

This book will be a tremendous help to those looking for faith, hope, love, and peace in whatever burden they carry as a cross. It will strengthen and provide them with an example of courage that they, in turn, will recognize in themselves; and then their own life experiences will show them that they are not alone. I only wish that more books that can convey the raw emotion that Jeannie demonstrates in this work would be published to help those who struggle to make sense of suffering, grief, and loss without providing just a clinical explanation, which can be helpful but is inadequate in helping them cope with some of the greatest mysteries of life.

—Rev. Stephen A. Thompson
Pastor of Holy Family and St. Thomas Parishes
Diocese of Springfield, Illinois

Acknowledgments

Before I became an author, I was told how many different people and talents are necessary before the finished book gets into the hands of readers. However, I never truly appreciated that fact until I began this odyssey with the book you are holding. *From Grief to Grace* began more as a concept than a book, and for the way it materialized into what you are reading, there are many people to whom I am indebted for their contributions, encouragement, and expertise. While this is by no means an exhaustive list, these are the people to whom I owe deep gratitude.

First, I could never have created this book without the prayers and encouragement from my dear friend and mentor, Eileen Benthal. Her exact words before I embarked on writing this book were, "You are supposed to write a book about grief, and it's supposed to be called *From Grief to Grace*." This was something she said to me with certainty after praying for me one day.

Shortly thereafter, my *Catholic Exchange* editor, Michael Lichens, asked me a simple question when I submitted a monthly article for publication on the site: "Have you ever thought of writing a book?" Once the question was asked, I more seriously considered the answer and began to pray for clear discernment. Michael was my editor for this book as well, and his patience, kindness, and clear direction are the reason the finished product you are reading is better than my original first draft of the manuscript. I owe Charlie McKinney incredible thanks as well for believing in this book enough to publish it.

I cannot end my acknowledgments without mentioning my family. My husband, Ben, is the silent supporter who rarely gets a nod of the head when I write an article, let alone a book. But Ben believed in this book and its message, and he not only offered moral support, but he also sacrificed countless hours of his free time watching our young girls with special abilities so that I could craft the manuscript. It has been a labor of love, and all of the incredible talent at Sophia Institute Press combined to fine-tune the editing, formatting, and design of the book you read now.

Without the many parts, a body could not function as a whole. Likewise, without the behind-the-scenes dedication of everyone involved in producing this book, it wouldn't exist. Above all, I must thank God for the gift He has given me, which I hope reaches many hearts and changes lives.

From Grief to Grace

Prologue

As a young child, I would ponder questions pertaining to eternity, questions many adults ask much later in life: *Who is God? Why did He create me? What purpose do I serve on this earth?* Often these musings occurred in the solitude of my childhood bedroom while I immersed myself in books and music that drew me into an eremitic mindset. Strangely—or providentially, as it happened—these thoughts and questions did not seem unusual in my five-year-old mind. They were natural and logical to me.

During one of my many contemplative reflections, I noticed a burning in my heart, a longing to do great things for God one day. I prayed that He would grant me the fortitude necessary to engage myself and others in this lifelong endeavor to know Him, to understand His love, to appreciate beauty and extend humble gratitude for His mercy. It was a pining born in a young girl's heart, fostered only by the fulfillment of searching, wrestling with deep questions, agonizing over the mysteries of human suffering, and battling with my own human inclinations toward comfort and sensory pleasures.

My first encounter with death and suffering was when my Uncle Ken died of lung cancer when I was only eight years old. His death was the first that truly impacted me, one that I recall with intense clarity to this day. Although he lived far from my family, his visits were meaningful. As a child, I sensed the urgency in facing his own mortality and in making every moment count by loving those whom God placed in his life, but I did not fully comprehend the articulation of these emotions or completely grasp the full extent of his—or my—suffering.

Following Uncle Ken's untimely death, I lost my beloved dog, who had truly become a member of our family. Swizzle was seventeen years old when she died, and she was the only pet who had been with our family from its origin. Our home became hollow after we buried her in the backyard, and the loss was intensely painful and nearly unbearable for me.

As a thirteen-year-old, I was beginning to recognize that life didn't fit into a predestined box. The stride of life was not simple, easy, or predictable. Life was messy, complicated, and confusing, not just because I was an adolescent, but because the burning to know and love God ran deeply in my veins and in the alcoves of my heart and soul. It encompassed every fiber of my existence, and so human suffering quickly entered the forefront of my mind.

To lose another family member in high school from medical complications related to years of heavy drug abuse was another blow to my fragile heart. I ruminated. I wept. I cried out in anger to the silence in my bedroom. I asked God, *Why? How could this happen?* I did not want to participate in suffering. Instead I wanted to flee from it as far as was humanly possible. Denial became a constant temptation to me. I imagined that if only I could pretend that I wasn't hurting and everything was fine, then surely it would be.

Suffering always seemed so contradictory to the life that was encouraged in the subtle underpinnings of 1990s American culture and society. Suffering was to be avoided, discouraged, and extinguished. Suffering indicated the presence of evil. Suffering meant death—literally or figuratively.

I, like the rest of the human race, did not want to suffer.

Since those early days, my life has been peppered with myriad losses, ranging from death to estranged relationships, the loss of a beloved career to moving to an entirely new region. I lost myself when I got married and had to navigate the loss of the single life while simultaneously embracing married life. I lost another aspect of my selfish nature when my children were born; life changed from filling my time with whatever I wanted to do each day to the demands of needy infants (and infants with special needs at that).

I knew and loved people who suffered from various addictions, psychological diagnoses, spiritual darknesses, and physical maladies. Grief afflicted nearly every aspect of my life, and, for a time, it was all I knew.

Yet I knew so little about grief itself. At the time, I pushed it away when it flooded my thoughts and gripped my emotions. I was angry that it took so long for me to move forward when lingering questions about life, death, and eternity were chiefly and constantly occupying my consciousness. I mistakenly assumed that my sorrow was actually clinical depression or some other, black-and-white diagnosis. My experiences seemed contrary to the proverbial American Dream, which I was overtly attempting to pursue in my young-adult years.

Yet I grappled with grief. It haunted me with its mysterious emergences, and all I wanted was for the nightmares to end so my fairytale could begin, as I had planned.

The most profound and poignant turning point in my understanding of grief occurred when our younger daughter, Sarah, was born in March 2013. My pregnancy had been healthy, and I enjoyed it with a newfound joy at every turning point. I had no suspicions of our daughter being anyone other than the perfectly imagined baby girl I had conjured in my mind. I fantasized about our two girls growing up with an idyllic sisterhood, one for which I had always longed as a child and yet never enjoyed.

But my triumphant joy quickly soured once my family doctor announced that a cesarean section was necessary for her birth. I had been in labor for nearly twenty-four hours at the time and was exhausted, emotionally drained, and yet absolutely stricken with a paralytic fright of a c-section. It was the most dreaded fear I have had to face to this day. Yet in that moment, in which I truly felt God had abandoned me, a voice from within said with certain clarity, *Say a prayer to Father Solanus Casey.*

It was an interior illumination in the midst of the darkest of moments. I offered a silent prayer as the medical staff prepped me for the cesarean. My body was no longer my own; I was strapped to a table with my arms secured, and I was completely numb from the waist down. Voluntary movement of my lower extremities was an impossibility. I recall thinking, in between tears, "It is as if I am in the position for crucifixion." So I imagined Jesus abandoning Himself to the Roman soldiers, and I wept privately.

Suddenly, however, my entire being was flooded with peace, following my quick cry for help to the Venerable Solanus Casey. I knew my guardian angel or the Holy Spirit had led me to So-lanus Casey's intercession, and my fear was transformed into a splendorous joy in this mysterious waiting and dramatic turning point of events.

No one knew my prayer, except God and the Heavenly Hosts. I told not a soul, not even my husband, Ben. When the on-call obstetrician delivered Sarah, the room fell silent as she heartily cried to announce her entrance into this world. I was relieved to hear that her lungs were strong, but I saw the concern on Ben's face as I was being stitched up after the operation.

There has never been a moment before or since in my life when I was rendered completely helpless. I couldn't even see my daughter. I couldn't touch her or hold her, yet my heart ached to understand what was happening.

Ben gently told me, "Her hands look like the fingers are fused together, and there's something wrong with her forehead." I sobbed. He hastily added with his ever-present optimism, "But I'm sure it's just because you had such a hard delivery. Maybe Sarah's facial features will soften after a while."

My maternal instinct knew this wasn't the case, and yet through my tears of uncertainty, this interior peace remained unfazed within my heart. Divine grace carried me through those initial days while I was convalescing in the hospital, because I saw Sarah's perceived birth defects, and yet I loved her. Ben and I wept together as the pediatrician shared her suspicions of a rare genetic condition called Apert Syndrome.

When Ben Googled it, we cried harder: a lifetime of corrective surgeries and a deformed face? This was our—and Sarah's —future?

Upon arriving home, we were thrust into a world we neither desired nor expected: crisis management. In addition to our adjusting to having a newborn in our family and my recovering from major surgery, we were suddenly making frantic phone calls and diagnostic appointments multiple times per day.

We had minimal time to process this emotional rollercoaster. We had entered survival mode and were determined to understand Sarah's diagnosis and prognosis. It was all that mattered, in addition to helping our older daughter, Felicity, adjust to having a baby sister in the house.

The first two weeks were a blur, and I was enshrouded in a particular darkness in which nothing made sense; all I could do was ask God all the questions we ask when someone dies: *Why? Why did this happen to me, to our family? Why Sarah? Why can't we just have a normal life like everyone else?*

I haplessly and wearily dragged myself to my two-week postpartum appointment with the on-call obstetrician who had delivered Sarah—the second time in my life I had ever seen the woman. The appointment, however, uplifted and comforted me, although it did not remove my unbearable agony. Dr. Annan told me that the delivery experience with Sarah was unforgettable to her. She was amazed at how flawlessly the cesarean went, as if it were performed with textbook precision. She marveled at how, despite Sarah's condition, she never needed to go to the NICU. But most notably, Dr. Annan told me she felt the hand of God deliver Sarah.

"It was as if something took over my hands as I was delivering Sarah from your womb. Someone took over. It felt as if God's hand, not mine, delivered your baby. I will never forget that."

Through tears mixed with bewilderment and appreciation, I smiled and thanked her. She continued, "Everything that happened in that operating room was miraculous. Every member of the medical staff who was present in that room remarked at how there seemed to be this incredible light in the room, a supernatural light. And we all noticed how you and your husband responded to Sarah. We agreed that you both were either Christians or in denial."

I didn't quite know how to respond to these comments at the time, because I was overwhelmed with conflicting emotions. But Dr. Annan spoke to me with confidence, with certainty. She did not waver in her belief that God was present, that God delivered Sarah, and that the event was miraculous.

"Your daughter is a special child of God," she concluded as we parted ways, and I reiterated my gratitude to her.

Grief suddenly became an acute awareness to me. I realized that my internal and external manifestations of emotional peaks and periods of sadness mingled with hope were actually the complexity of grief. And the grief over losing the daughter I thought we would have suddenly morphed into the relief that, although Sarah was different and would always be different, she was still very much alive and such a happy little girl.

So I mourned my dreams, my expectations, and my hopes for a time. I permitted myself to encounter the process of grieving without censorship, and yet it was a lonely journey. It was often perplexing and grievous to navigate, difficult to explain and multidimensional in its manifestations.

Over the course of almost a year, the Lord revealed to me the vision for this book. It's not a manual, not a self-help journal. It is not a guideline or even, truthfully, a pure memoir. It is a conglomeration of my life experience mingled with my understanding of human suffering, its meaning and purpose, and the spiritual, emotional, and physical implications of grieving.

Life has an interesting way of putting things into perspective. I have never been the type of person who prefers small talk and chitchat to real, honest, authentic dialogue. Because of this, people typically open up to me fairly easily and quickly. In listening to their stories, my heart has gathered the very raw and powerful emotions that often accompany a person's journey of sorrow.

More and more, I am observing the despair and despondency that often define people's suffering. In conversations with others,

I listen to their woeful stories, and my heart often breaks with theirs. They share with me stories of children who have died, of surviving cancer but losing a loved one to it, of feeling lost and uncertain as to their identity, of deciphering a healthy balance between their own boundaries and self-respect while loving those who suffer from addiction. There are many other examples, but I realized the need for all of us to discover that life has value in all of its forms and stages, even in the midst of the darkest of moments.

I have learned that most of us do not recall the mediocre or even the splendid moments of achievement and utter bliss we have experienced. What tends to make the most significant impression on us are the intense sufferings and losses that have defined our life's journey, most especially when we have deepened our character or noticed ways in which we have overcome our myriad adversities.

I have collected these stories from people from all walks of life, and they have become permanently emblazoned in my mind's eye. I have heard countless stories of lives lost—to war, disease, political upheaval, martyrdom, suicide, murder, addiction. I have heard of grievous and intensely painful losses—of homes, careers, dreams, relationships, and financial hardships.

There are children who are born with rare genetic conditions, like my daughter, who will undergo dozens of surgeries over the course of their lifetimes. There are children younger than mine who are afflicted with incurable cancers and die prematurely. I've been told of miscarriages, stillbirths, infertility, and the longing for filling a home with the laughter and love of children.

As people shared their tales of woe with me, they often asked me questions that have no definitive answer or solution: *Why did this happen? How could a benevolent God permit something so horrific to happen to a child? My father was a good person, always doing the right thing; why did he have to suffer for years before he died? Why does death exist? How can I get over this?*

Over time, it occurred to me that a book on grief from a spiritual viewpoint, supplemented with my personal anecdotes, might benefit innumerable people. There are many obvious and pertinent reasons for this:

• *Grief is universal and does not discriminate.* It does not select people of a particular race, socioeconomic status, religion, or culture. All people of all eras have experienced heartache, betrayal, loss of a loved one through death, divorce, or separation; chaos, crisis, or change. Grief is a language all people understand; it is a language of tragedy and (hopefully) eventual resilience.

Because all of us emote typically difficult feelings associated with grief—sorrow, confusion, stress, anger, darkness, sadness, frustration—it is a type of language of the heart that we all speak and understand. It unites all of humanity.

It is also a contradiction, because grief is both a blessing and a burden. It is complex and multifaceted, fluid rather than chronological. It affects and afflicts all of us to varying degrees throughout our lifetimes.

• *No one is exempt from grief.* It is, quite simply, a significant aspect of the human condition. We are born into sin and are perpetually affected by sin until (or unless) we enter the beatific vision in the afterlife. All of creation reflects God's glory, but it also weeps with the universal effects of sin. Even if our lives were nearly flawless and perfect, we would still encounter evil and disease in our environment, if nowhere else.

• *Life is a mystery.* It is in the mystery of the unknown, the unanswered questions, the silence with which we are often met in the most desperate of prayers, where we discover who we are and where we are going. In the darkness, we must honestly face ourselves and consider the possibilities to our rhetorical questions about our existence and purpose.

Recognizing, understanding, and navigating our grief can transform the way we view the world and the way we approach what we are incapable of controlling. We truly can discover a lasting interior peace if we traverse this journey as a community of seekers who carry the confidence and hope that we will reach our destinations and one day discover the ultimate joy that awaits us.

Following many long conversations, hours of prayer and discernment, and over a year of realizing my personal mission as a direct result of my compounded grief, this book has materialized. My hope and prayer is that it will reach you wherever you are in the process of bereavement and that something will speak to the depths and recesses of your heart to rekindle the light that you may have lost or that may have weakened over time.

There is hope, even and especially in the darkest of times.

My ultimate desire is that this book will bring hope to those who grieve. Since grief touches all of our lives and virtually no one is exempt from suffering, sorrow, and eventual death, it is a subject that must be tackled, however messy it may appear. Grief is often approached as a taboo topic, and most of us do not know how to respond to those who grieve, much less to differentiate clearly between grief and something else going on in our own lives.

Perhaps this book will teach us that there is much life to be lived in the midst of loss and change. Perhaps we will learn that all things work together for good, that God can somehow transform our grief into a means of helping others and journeying with them in their own pain. Perhaps it will be a beacon of light in the midst of a dark world.

One final thought before we begin this journey together: I am no *formal* expert on this topic. Although I do have a background in psychology and counseling, I am just like you in many ways—sifting through bouts of anger and confusion, setbacks, irritations, and frustrations while occasionally receiving glimpses of joy and peace in the midst of an otherwise chaotic life. You and I are walking different—but parallel—paths, and this book is where our lives intersect, if only for a time.

Thank you for choosing to travel with me, to invite my story into yours so that the interior tumult may temporarily cease as we encounter the shower of blessings that awaits us.

1

The Complexity of Human Suffering

I remember the first time I was officially introduced to the five stages of grief. I was sitting in an undergraduate elective course, entitled "Introduction to Moral Theology." It was a two-hundred-level class, one that I predetermined would be a bore and a blow-off and yet might perk up my transcript once I entered the working world of adults. The five-hundred-page textbook loudly thumped as I hefted it onto my squeaky and awkward desk that was certain to be a remnant from the first renovations of the college in the 1960s.

I had no desire to open the book. It was uninviting, clinically written, and particularly insipid. I knew this before I ever bothered to read one page. I chose to go to college so that my thinking might be challenged, my character deepened. I was thirsting for *authentic opportunities* at critical thinking and analyses, but most of my religious-studies minor courses were unimpressive at best, pathetic and pitiful at worst. I was only a junior in college and had pretty much mentally checked out. I know I did during this class, because it was a rudimentary and somewhat insulting perspective of morality. I was longing for something more, a class that would ignite reflection, deeper self-awareness, and meaningful encounter with the eternal.

I'm not certain whether my professor assumed his students were apathetic or averse toward the course topic, but he certainly taught it as if neither he nor we cared to delve into deeper questions about the mysteries of life, death, and human suffering. Most of the time it seemed as if I was back in elementary school, memorizing and regurgitating definitions rather than constructively piecing together complex concepts that would somehow weave their way into my psyche and soul for further contemplation.

Dr. Loving attempted to rally the students as he forced a smile on his robust face. "Okay, everyone, so far we haven't covered much material in the textbook, and I think this will be the perfect way to introduce the contents we need to cover before the semester ends."

We were nearing midterms, and I still hadn't bothered to read my $250 textbook. I had convinced myself that the exorbitant amounts of money I was spending on required texts was a complete rip-off, especially since I had to work for two weeks just to earn enough to purchase one book. Yet I couldn't bear to read the book on my own, since our exams and essays rarely covered the highlighted and emboldened terms in it.

As you can see, I am not a natural optimist, and my pessimism was surging at this point in the class.

Dr. Loving began furiously scribbling on the chalkboard:

The Five Stages of Grief:
1. Denial
2. Anger
3. Bargaining
4. Depression
5. Acceptance

The Complexity of Human Suffering

These stages have been the standard of understanding and explaining grief to students and counselors, pastors and educators for decades, generally without dispute or refutation. In her bestselling classic, *On Death and Dying: What the Dying Have to Teach Doctors, Nurses, Clergy and Their Own Families*, Elisabeth Kübler-Ross and her colleagues passionately researched and then identified what we now call the "stages of grief": denial, anger, bargaining, depression, and acceptance.

We opened our books to discover a mere two pages explaining Kübler-Ross's theory about grief and loss, and at this point in my life, I just accepted her ideology without question. It was logical and conclusive. I wanted to pass my exam and get out of this course. I had my mind and heart set on greater things at the time.

"Can anyone explain what grief is?" Dr. Loving painfully asked, and I mused that the question seemed impossible to answer fully, so, of course, no one responded.

After clearing his throat, he continued, "Grief is the process we experience when someone dies. It is our reaction to the loss. We will briefly cover Elisabeth Kübler-Ross's model and stages of grief, which will be included in the exam ..."

His voice trailed off as I starred the chicken scratchings I had made in my notebook. I read the page where my book lay open. *Denial*: this is the first stage of grief, whereby a person learns initially to cope with the loss incurred. Most people begin with denial, because they cannot face the gravity of the loss. Instead, they ignore the reality and continue on with their lives as if everything were normal.[1]

---

[1] This is paraphrased from my memory of the textbook we used in my "Introduction to Catholic Theology" class. Of course, the textbook is now obsolete and out of print.

Hmm, I pondered as Dr. Loving continued his weak treatise on this weary introduction. *That makes sense, I suppose.*

Anger: the second stage of grief that occurs following a person's initial experience of denial, in which rage and resentment or even regret surfaces.[2] I nodded in agreement, and I repeated this blind acknowledgment through the remaining three stages of grief.

Bargaining, according to Kübler-Ross, is the third stage of grief and occurs when a person attempts to plead with God: *If only you grant me . . . then I will . . . Depression* happens when the loss becomes unbearable, and a person succumbs to its weight and the reality that what has happened can never be reversed. Finally, *acceptance* ensues when the person does not fight the loss and understands the reality of what has happened while resting peacefully with that reality.

For decades, this was the extent of Western society's view on grief and loss. It nearly became commonplace to teach this theory and not refute it or analyze it for its veracity. No one questioned its pragmatism or rationale, because it appealed quite nicely to human logic. Even when I took "Maturing and Aging" as a course requirement for my psychology undergraduate degree, the five stages were briefly presented with no other model or understanding of human suffering.

While Kübler-Ross's extensive work on the subject is impressive, I have found in my own life experience that it falls short of embodying the complete image of human loss and sorrow. Most

---

[2] The explanation of each classical stage of grief is paraphrased and based on both the textbook we used in my "Introduction to Catholic Theology" class, as well as from Kübler-Ross's best seller, *On Death and Dying.*

people mistakenly assume that Kübler-Ross believed these stages were chronological, that people experienced first denial, then anger, and so on. Many psychologists today acknowledge that some people pass through one stage and may regress to a previous one or never experience a particular stage at all. For example, one person may never reach acceptance and simply remain in the other stages or perhaps vacillate between anger and denial for an extended period.

To her credit, Kübler-Ross admitted the limitations to her theory, explaining that her five stages were initially collected to describe a specific population of those experiencing grief: the terminally ill. She never intended for her five-stages theory to be adopted as a universally applicable belief system for anyone in bereavement.[3] However, most psychology majors in the early 2000s were unfortunately not exposed to the limitations of her theory. By the time I reached college, my professors had universally incorporated her five-stages theory into an assumed generalization that appealed to logic but not to experience.

The intent here is not to trivialize Kübler-Ross's highly acclaimed research that has remained largely substantiated through decades of counselors' and psychologists' work with those in mourning. Rather, the hope is to illustrate how we often subconsciously and automatically accept ideologies, such as the five-stages-of-grief theory, without researching their origins and intended applications. This is one subject in which we must not blindly espouse a philosophy simply because experts in a certain industry have confidently advised us to do so.

---

[3] Kübler-Ross developed these stages of grief, which she explains in great detail in her book *On Death and Dying*, as they related to the subjects of her studies, who were terminally ill patients.

Grief experts tend also to purport mistakenly that grief is restricted to the death of a loved one. This is, at least in part, why so many people are bewildered when they hear of someone who is feeling grief when they lose a job or receive a devastating diagnosis or—as in my case—gives birth to a child who suffers from a rare and chronic genetic condition. From a societal perception, grief and death are mutually inclusive at all times.

In addition, the first image that comes to mind when we hear the word *grief* is death. It seems as if the two are synonymous, based on our postmodern culture's viewpoint. But we have a different vantage, because our lens as Catholic Christians extends beyond the here-and-now and ourselves. We see things from an angle imbued with divine grace. Therefore, the meaning of grief and its implications in our lives (both individual and universal) include but are not limited to death. Instead, we are transformed by and through all types of loss through redemptive suffering and, ultimately, resurrection.

Although people mean well, their comments often come across as callous and hollow when we are in the throes of sorrow. Many well-intentioned acquaintances stopped by our house shortly after Sarah's birth and asked how I was managing. I always found this to be a loaded question, one for which most people did not truly desire an honest and complete response. So I would smile and slowly nod, purposefully replying with something ambiguous, such as, "I'm hanging in there okay. It's tough, but I'm trying to keep my head above water."

Naturally, most people accept this type of response at face value, but they also like to add their two cents' worth of wisdom. "Well, count your blessings. At least she wasn't stillborn." Still others would chime in, "You are so blessed, because God gives special children to special parents." One person even asked me,

The Complexity of Human Suffering

"Why would you be sad? It's not like your daughter died or any-thing. Remember, there are children who are dying of cancer in the world."

I was cognitively and keenly aware of these kernels of truths (except for the God-gives-special-children-to-special-parents bit). But as the comments compounded over time, I realized that our culture and society hold a very superficial comprehension of suffering and loss. In turn, I internalized my emotions and played the game of social etiquette with a courteous-yet-clichéd reply to people's questions about my ability to tackle the world of crisis management.

It was during these very raw and sensitive weeks and months when Sarah was an infant that it struck me how inadequate—and even insulting—were the five stages of grief that I long ago mem-orized and to which I blindly acquiesced.

Grief was not chronological at all to me, and perhaps this is true for most people. It was complex, confusing, and multidi-mensional. It was fluid and often indefinable. It was occurring at both the conscious and subconscious levels, and new dis-coveries constantly surfaced and then went dormant, only to resurface again. I was constantly learning and relearning about myself—who I was, why this was happening, and how I was supposed to respond to it all.

Grief is also not limited to five simple stages. Certainly we have encountered every one of the five points in Kübler-Ross's model in our own journeys, and yet these explanations seemed all too parsimonious and generalized to me. They tend to be more frustrating than informative, and this only exacerbates our sense of loneliness and isolation when what we are truly seeking is companionship, camaraderie, and relief in the form of community.

From Grief to Grace

I first became cognizant of these manifestations of grief only after Sarah was born. The first two weeks postpartum were agonizing to me. I entered a spiritual darkness that was entirely unfamiliar to me. Nothing made sense, and my lamentations to God became redundant and emotionally draining after a while. I felt angry that my friends were all giving birth to perfectly healthy, typical babies while Sarah was afflicted with an incurable, lifelong syndrome, but I was concurrently weeping at the loss of what I had hoped our life would be with two daughters.

Shame became an uninvited guest as I was faced with the reality that I wanted to hide Sarah from the world so that people would not whisper and stare at us. I was hoping to avoid becoming a mockery in our community. Often I felt all of these emotions in conjunction with a bizarre glimmer of hope or wellspring of relief when people blessed us with unexpected holy hours or heartfelt and prophetic words of encouragement.

These emotions overwhelmed me and swallowed me whole. At night, I would toss and turn, wrestling with my inner turmoil, unwilling and not yet ready to release them to God's providential care. I clung to the darkness with the vain hope that, by my attempt to control and further isolate myself and my family, life wouldn't present me with any more surprises or mayhem.

In that darkness and in that wrestling, I was often tempted to give up, just to exist and go through the motions of living, to represent myself and our family as rising above and thriving in the midst of the unknown. It seemed easier to give in to the world's perception of how I should live my life and how I should handle Sarah's diagnosis rather than present God with my own fiat to His plans for my life, His hopes and dreams for me.

At one point it became evident to me that we are all given a choice in the midst of grief: victim or victory. As victims, we can claim our right to dwell in perpetual self-pity, creating a sphere of codependence and relative ease in moving through the monotony and routine of every day. As victims, we don't need to explain ourselves to anyone, because we are sure to be veiled in an unspoken understanding among friends and acquaintances who know our stories. As victims, hardly anything is required of us at all.

But in choosing victory, we choose tenacity. We choose resilience. We determine our destinies and move forward in hope and in the confident composure of placing one foot in front of the other without needing to know the outcome of every detail in our lives. Victory means that we are capable of achieving great things with God's blessing and grace. Victory means that we become a living testimony that death is not the end, but only the beginning of new life. And death includes physical but also spiritual and emotional death, as in the dying to self so necessary for obtaining that prevailing peace within.

Interior death is hidden to the world and yet is the very antithesis to self-aggrandizement. Sometimes God strips us to a spiritual nakedness or emotional transparency, which leaves us feeling vulnerable and exposed. We are afraid to die in this way, and yet when we become empty of self, we are open and available for God to fill our nothingness with an abundance of spiritual fruitfulness that defies explanation.

This poverty of spirit is quite different from the emptiness brought on by sin or circumstance. A soul can feel God removing particular emotional or temporal attachments, which often seems like pruning or tearing away the distractions to which we desperately cling. This stripping to a place of spiritual vacancy often occurs spontaneously and in conjunction with a deepening of one's interior life. A person's desires may expand from merely living a comfortable life to being drawn to a radical holiness that only God can construct, but this construction of Himself within a soul can happen only with the destruction of self and ego.

With this illustration, a person can clearly see how this is different from feeling lonely or alone. While a soul that is being interiorly rebuilt may honestly feel alone, lost, and lonely at times, the spiritual fruit of peace, faithfulness, and joy are magnanimously present and available. The soul nearly rejoices in its lament over all it has lost because of all it is gaining through God's love.

I chose victory. I chose to believe that God has something to teach all of us — an important lesson about life, love and loss, and ultimately about dying to our concupiscence so that we can rise (both literally and metaphorically) in His glory and grace. Although suffering is a critical component to learning this life lesson, it is not the ultimate end. The end result is light, love, and hope, mercy and grace. It is a message that the Lord desires to extend to us all if we are willing to take the risk in suffering for the sake of love.

Grief or Depression?

When death and significant loss touch our lives, grief may masquerade as depression, but the two are divergent in subtle ways. If prolonged grief deters us from reentering life and finding goodness in what is left without that person or situation or job that is now gone, depression may (or may not) be the root cause. There is no panacea for this. Our bodies and minds are incredibly inimitable, so the only way to determine what may be causing a long-term shift in our behavior is through medical and psychological evaluations. It's also valuable to weigh the alternative possibilities, including the often abstruse ways that grief peeks and pokes into our lives through emotions, thoughts, and behaviors. Differentiating between grief and depression may offer the aggrieved individual a basis of understanding when, how, and where to obtain additional help.

I looked up at our family physician with desperation, tears pooling in my eyes. I spoke quietly and avoided eye contact with him purposefully. I knew I was risking much by my emotional vulnerability, but I truly did not know what else to do. I had reached a breaking point, a point at which I knew something was amiss with my life, but I could not pinpoint it. Out of exasperation, I reached out to the only "experts" to whom I had access: medical professionals.

"Have you thought about medication for depression, Jeannie?"

He asked me apprehensively, seemingly out of a fear of my potential response, although he wasn't unkind. My physician appeared sympathetic, yet it was clear that he was diagnosing me through a purely medical lens rather than holistically taking into account my entire life.

I paused for longer than what is considered socially acceptable and then sighed heavily. "I have, doctor, and yet I know I do not have clinical depression."

Naturally, he offered me a furtive glance—not out of concurrence with my statement, but rather out of a blithe submission, most likely having heard this tale time and again from those whom he may have considered to be the typical "neurotic housewives." I knew it was futile to convince him otherwise. It was written in his countenance: a slight furrow of the brow, a subtle nod, and a quick purse of the lips.

"I see," he finally responded. "And why don't you think it is clinical depression?" he challenged.

I knew my refutation of his assumption seemed arrogant and naive, as my educational background was in psychology, but it was something I intuited, a kind of imperceptible knowledge hidden somewhere in my soul. I wondered if it was the Holy Spirit nudging me as He so often did in the most inconvenient of places and times.

"Well, I just need to figure out what might help me. Diet and nutrition? Supplements? Counseling perhaps?" My voice weakened as I considered my options.

He didn't have to say the word *medication* before my mind conjured up thousands of reasons why I simply would not consider psychotropic medication for this particular excerpt of my life.

Was it some unresolved, painful memories of my childhood in which I saw the effects of medication on a child, then an adolescent, then a young adult? It all seemed like an experiment to discover the correct dosage and type of pill that suited my younger brother's needs. It was no one's fault. But all I could see in my mind's eye was my brother, sobbing to himself in his bedroom when he believed no one could see or hear him, pleading and begging with God to remove this nightmare from his life.

Was it because I understood the effects of medication on the brain? During my undergraduate days, I had opted to take "Introduction to Physiological Psychology" as an elective, which was both fascinating and informative. It was then I learned about how psychotropic medication alters the neurotransmitters (chemical substances) in brains that are either lacking or produce too much of a particular neurotransmitter substance (NTS). I also knew that psychotropic medications could alter the way the brain behaved, and their permanent effects (side effects or otherwise) were unknown.

Psychotropic medication does truly help some people cope with a psychological diagnosis. As a counselor, I worked with people who had various diagnoses and managed well on both the proper dose and type of psychotropic medication. I knew the effects of SSRIs and MAOIs[4] on the brain and how calming they could be for people who genuinely suffered from common psychological ailments. But was this a psychological diagnosis—or something else?

It felt like something else, something visceral and even spiritual. Part of my reticence was due to my intuitive nature: that gut feeling that nagged at me when something wasn't quite on target. That's how it felt while I momentarily considered his viewpoint.

I swallowed my pride and cleared my throat. "Doctor, I just know. I don't feel comfortable taking psychotropic medication, and it's not because I am too proud to admit I have a problem. I just know I don't have depression."

With that, he sighed, shook his head, and said, "Jeannie, sometimes people who are very versed in a particular field, as you are in psychology, can be very stubborn about these types of issues. In fact, it's very likely that you are not capable of looking at this objectively."

I didn't judge him. I wasn't taken aback. In fact, I found his straightforward approach to be refreshing and appealing. But I still didn't agree with him.

Yes, I am stubborn. I am also persistent. I don't go against my intuition. It doesn't bode well for the consequences that are sure to ensue.

---

[4] SSRIs are selective serotonin reuptake inhibitors that are used to treat Major Depressive Disorder, and MAOIs are monoamine oxidase inhibitors, which are prescribed to those who are diagnosed with depression or Bipolar Disorder. MAOIs are older forms of antidepressants, while SSRIs are more commonly used today.

"Okay, well, thanks anyway. I just wanted to see if you knew of any alternative ways I might be able to deal with some of my symptoms. It's just not normal for me, that's all."

He shrugged and dismissed me by saying, "The symptoms you describe are too vague and could apply to a number of origins, including depression," he added with emphasis.[5]

I didn't overlook his point, but I departed the office feeling discouraged and defeated once again. I was left with a myriad of questions still unanswered, and my energy was waning—not just for the day, but for the week.

You see, I told my physician about my daily life, but he already knew about Sarah's condition and was at least nominally aware of Felicity's sensory issues and anxiety. I explained that I was skittish all the time at home, that I couldn't sleep an entire night without waking up with heart palpitations, and that I frequently broke out in a cold sweat and lost my temper on a daily basis. The headaches were persistent, and the nausea was unlike early stages of pregnancy. It was a general feeling of burnout that began to cause physical symptoms of undefined sickness in my body.

My hunch: stress and grief; his (unofficial) diagnosis: clinical depression.

---

[5] Indeed, my family physician had a point I initially overlooked. Since that appointment, I've discovered I have a few autoimmune diseases, and most of the symptoms I experienced were due to the undiagnosed illnesses that were festering in my body, undetected. It's important to note that both psychological and purely physiological conditions can include symptoms that overlap. Ambiguity in conventional medicine is a clear frustration to both the patient and the attending physician. This is why it's critical to know your body's reactions to stress, food, medications, and so forth and to continue seeking professional help in the form of both counseling and medical clinicians.

The Complexity of Human Suffering

What is clinical depression, anyway? The newest edition of the *Diagnostic and Statistical Manual of Mental Disorders*, or the DSM-V, has redefined this phenomenon as major depressive disorder.[6] Many may relate to my vignette above: the doctor's visit, the diagnosis of depression, and the gut feeling that it's just not right. It's something else, but we automatically adopt the labels we are handed by experts and professionals.

It's crucial to follow your intuition while concurrently seeking medical expertise, which may lead you to take medication. It's not just a bizarre, unverified notion that is somehow tenuous enough to consider mere positive thinking, but rather it is the way in which the Holy Spirit speaks to you—in the innermost crevices of your heart, soul, and mind that work in conjunction with each other to lead you to the truth about yourself.[7]

Major depressive disorder (MDD) and grief are two entirely different phenomena, although they do have characteristics that overlap. For one, grief is very fluid and can occur in unexpected ways or manifest itself intensely or more subtly in a person's psyche. Major depressive disorder requires consistent, pervasive physiological and psychological symptoms over a period of two consecutive weeks or longer; the criteria include suicidal ideations (e.g., thinking), excessive weight loss or gain, energy loss

---

6 The DSM-V or *Diagnostic and Statistical Manual of Mental Disorders*, fifth revision, includes the newest information about psychological diagnoses and is based on research and interpretation of the research of members of the American Psychiatric Association.

7 This type of self-awareness is developed and matured through close connection to the sacraments and often through spiritual direction. It's impossible for us to form our own consciences without proper formation from the Magisterium.

and fatigue, feelings of worthlessness, irritable mood, inability to concentrate, and change in sleep patterns.

Grief, however, does not consistently exhibit the same characteristics in these ways. Most of us experience grief in bouts of intense anger that may persist for a day or a couple of days, perhaps a week. We may undergo a wave of loneliness or sadness, an inability to relate to other "typical" people. But these often come and go as rhythmically as ocean waves crash onto the shore. Grief ebbs and flows. We may believe we have "gotten over" our mourning, and then suddenly we hear a song that triggers a memory or we see a photograph or walk into a person's home. Our senses remind us that grief remains latent, but somehow we are capable of muddling through our daily lives and even discovering — or rediscovering — its meaning, purpose, value, and joy.

Grief is not classified in the same way major depressive disorder is, and whereas there may be demonstrable physiological changes in the brain that occur when we are in mourning, as there are definitively in MDD, grief does not follow any particular patterns in behavior. Although MDD is defined as the "common cold of mental illness" because of its prevalence in every society and culture and throughout virtually every recordable epoch, grief is nondiscriminate. In other words, grief presents itself to every human being, whereas not everyone is afflicted with MDD or some other, similar psychological ailment.

Sadly, the most common (and menial) definition of grief is "deep sadness" or "deep and poignant distress,"[8] usually precipitated by death. It's true that grief involves stark sadness or, more accurately, sorrow. Sadness is more qualitative of depres-

---

[8] *Merriam-Webster Dictionary*, s.v. "grief," accessed November 7, 2015, http://www.merriam-webster.com/dictionary/grief.

sion, while sorrow is more specific to grief, particularly grief that resides within a person at all times. However, this grief (unlike depression) isn't persistent sorrow, but instead it validates suffering as a gift and is elevated to a state of joy even when the person is deeply troubled by a loss of any kind.

When we do not process our grief adequately, we may enter into what is called complicated grief.[9] Complicated grief mimics major depressive disorder in that a person often feels worthless and excessively guilty, but in complicated grief the person will also obsess over the person who has died or the loss that has occurred, ruminate over the past, and be unable to focus on day-to-day activities of self-care. When grief becomes complicated, it's important to seek professional help, especially if suicidal ideations develop.

Of course, one could presumably—and accurately—point out that grief is nearly always complex, as mourning never occurs on a merely superficial level. When we grieve, our entire being suffers. Our senses remind us of the void through loss of appetite, tears welling up in our eyes, the sensation of a broken heart. We are fatigued. We are emotionally drained. Spiritually, our souls recognize the absence of a person or dream or pet or relationship

---

[9] The Mayo Clinic explains in its online article "Complicated Grief" that this phenomenon occurs when "feelings of loss are debilitating and don't improve even after time passes," so that resuming life as it was before the loss becomes impossible. Complicated grief is clinically defined as Persistent Complex Bereavement Disorder, which is when these symptoms severely interfere with one's daily activities accessed. "Complicated Grief," posted September 13, 2014, Mayo Clinic website, accessed October 26, 2015, http://www.mayoclinic.org/diseases-conditions/complicated-grief/basics/definition/con-20032765.

or job that once existed and is now permanently vanquished. The soul laments in the darkness that engulfs it for a time.

With the multiple layers of suffering that a person experiences—physiological changes and spiritual and emotional transformations—is it fair to say that all grief is, in fact, complicated grief? In theory, yes, but in order to differentiate the typical process of navigating our grief in a healthy manner versus the more morose and pervasive type of grief that may require professional help, it is crucial to separate the two clearly by definition.

It was only in recent years that I even remotely grasped the difference between grief and depression. My increasing frustration with medical and psychological experts on their persistence for prescribing me an antidepressant tugged at my heart to discover the depth and source of my pain. I got out of bed every day, took care of my hygienic needs and those of my daughters, made sure we were all well fed, warm, and learning something new. My interests were varied and vibrant. I sought new ways to understand the changing world and society, to connect with my neighbors, family, and friends. I noticed the gifts and blessings of each day.

This was clearly not depression. This was something entirely different. But when an otherwise ordinary day turned sour with only a comment from a well-meaning passerby or perhaps an awkward encounter from a stranger who gawked at Sarah in the grocery store, I would second-guess myself, and my confidence immediately diminished. The "what ifs" would suddenly cloud my ability to think soundly and discern my emotions pragmatically. I would return home from what I expected to be a normal outing and find myself sobbing uncontrollably while the girls took their afternoon naps.

The Complexity of Human Suffering

Why? How could this be? I awoke with a renewed appreciation for the sunshine and the verdant grass, the opportunity to start anew, and the excitement of waiting to see how the day would unfold. Yet halfway through the day, I found myself bemoaning over an otherwise trite encounter with someone I would most likely never see again.

So, in my bewilderment, I permitted myself to cry. All of us can allow the tears to cascade down our faces as they will. We pray for the wisdom to understand what triggers the intensity of this solitary emotional tirade. More often than not, we realize another layer of grief we have not yet experienced simply surfaced and made its way into our consciousness in order to make us aware of the mystery of suffering and how we might be able to offer it as an oblation to God for a greater purpose. Once we determine that our sorrow mingles with the love cradled in our hearts, the anger softly fades away. Then we dry our tears, smile, thank Jesus for this gift, and go on with our day.

Your experience with grief most likely looks nothing like mine, but the commonalities still offer some insight into the human experience. We are born with no expectation of goodness or evil, yet we encounter both immediately. We learn in ways both covert and explicit the certainty of betrayal, loneliness, physical pain, hunger, feeling tired, and the warmth of love and security.

Grief is one aspect of many that weaves itself into our overall experience of life. When we become attuned with our bodies, our souls, our thoughts and emotions, we grow in self-knowledge. This, in turn, draws us into a deeper empathy toward ourselves and others. We learn to be kind to ourselves when we are flooded with unexpected sorrow, and then we are capable of eventually sitting in silence with others who feel alone in their struggles and simply need a gentle, human presence, touch, or glance to offer them strength and comfort.

This is the silver lining of grief: that darkness and death are not the finalities, the punctuation at the end of a sentence. They do not define us. They do not control us. They simply intertwine with the joys of life, but they can (paradoxically) be tremendous blessings that eventually enrich our lives in ways that otherwise would not develop without the experience of transient sorrow.

A contemporary Christian song, "Just Be Held," by Casting Crowns[10] is reminiscent of the splendor hiding in the midst of ugliness, loss, and suffering:

> If your eyes are on the storm,
> You'll wonder if I love you still.
> But if your eyes are on the Cross,
> You'll know I always have and I always will.
>
> And not a tear is wasted.
> In time, you'll understand.
> I'm painting beauty with the ashes.
> Your life is in my hands.

Ashes symbolize the dust of our nothingness, for we were created from the dust and will return to it when we die (see Gen. 3:19). To consider that God paints a masterpiece of our lives with the ashes and dust that remain once we have loved and lost should be cause enough for rejoicing. Although we hear, "Remember you are dust, and to dust you shall return" on Ash Wednesday,

---

[10] Mark Hall, Bernie Herms, and Matthew West, "Just Be Held," performed by Casting Crowns (Sony/ATV Tree Publishing 2013).

we can ponder the meaning of repentance and conversion as we grieve. Grief activates something entirely new in us, which is an opportunity for metanoia,[11] or continual conversion. The *Catechism of the Catholic Church* perfectly explains this cusp of mystery in our lives: *animi cruciatus*, "affliction of spirit."[12] In her infinite wisdom, the Church describes some types of sadness as constructive. Grief propels us into a place of internal turmoil and immense sorrow, but that sorrow can be beneficial to our souls if we encounter it with a mindset open to the truths and mysteries of our Faith as it pertains to redemptive suffering. Grief, then, is merely one aspect of many in our journey to conversion and, eventually, to Heaven.

Although both grief and depression include inescapable sadness and possibly difficulty moving forward in our lives, the two phenomena are divergent in subtle but distinguishable ways. Depression as a diagnosis is widespread, probably because of the common, vague symptoms that could suggest an alternative primary diagnosis. Grief is a holistic experience that cannot be medically diagnosed unless prolonged periods of mourning do not improve with time. Both issues can—and should—be addressed not just from a psychological or medical standpoint but also from a spiritual angle so that comprehensive care can address the root cause of the symptoms.

Grief as a Taboo Topic in Modern Society
Most of us have probably encountered others who ask how we are feeling (or coping or "doing") when life becomes wearisome. Should we respond with the expected, "I'm doing fine, thanks" or

[11] From the Greek, "changing one's mind" or "repentance."
[12] See CCC 1431, based on Ezek. 36:26–27.

perhaps express honestly that we aren't okay? When we choose the latter, we may be met with a terse but courteous reply. Life experience reminds us that participating in or inviting an open, authentic dialogue is unacceptable when negative emotions are present. Only when we provide seemingly fluffy or vivacious answers to that question are we met with an invitation to share more.

We may ask ourselves, *Why are people uncomfortable with difficult emotions, such as sorrow, grief, and anger?*

There is no straightforward answer, of course, and naturally, generalizations never apply to everyone, but one can take a snippet of a situation or a microcosm of people and assume that a pattern does exist that can offer an explanation of human behavior.

Our culture is entirely uninviting to any expression of emotional or spiritual depth. Our society fears intimacy, unless it is physical intimacy. We are bombarded with messages both blatant and more understated about the types of lives that will draw us into a blissful existence. Perfectly sculpted bodies, perfectly white teeth, perfectly groomed hair, beautiful nails and clothes all apparently contribute to an overall satisfied sense of well-being. A well-kept home, perhaps a pet, a couple of kids, and a lucrative career will additionally provide satisfaction and a sense of completion in our lives.

This is the message of society. This has become our focus, our obsession—to appear perfectly put together and to maintain a level of busyness that will boost our chances of acquiring more wealth, recognition, and status. We base our lives on the goal of happiness. And we falsely pursue what our culture, rather than our Faith, advises us to find: that evasive sense of happiness.

Because of various forms of escapism, we tend to drown ourselves with constant noise and motion. Technology has overwhelmingly provided the instant-gratification platform to make the temptation for distraction an ever-present reality in our lives. Consider the cultural obsession with zombies, vampires, extraterrestrials, and the like, all of which are invading not only movie theaters and television, but also video games and music.

We desire the supernatural, but we tend to seek it through fantastical rather than genuine and realistic pathways. When we do this, we are silencing the opportunity to grow in self-knowledge, to encounter God as a Person, and to relate authentically to the people He places in our lives.

Our conversations with others are no different, be they with strangers or spouses. We don't dare discuss the raw and difficult thoughts and emotions that occupy most of our time. We don't seek counsel about the very real and very important matters pertaining to our connection to eternity: *Who is God? Why are we here? What is there after this life? How do we share our lives with God in eternity? What is love, and how can we love more profoundly? What do we do with the messy and complex suffering we experience?*

Society tells us to ignore and deny suffering, to run from it, to obliterate it as soon as it encroaches on our personal territory. We see this in the ways people respond to abnormal test results, whether it is a malignant tumor or a child with anencephaly. The subtle undercurrent is always to eliminate the struggle rather than to choose life instead of death (Deut. 30:19). The person with the tumor is advised to "die with dignity" through self-imposed euthanasia, while the couple with the child who will surely die only minutes outside of his mother's womb is strongly encouraged to terminate the pregnancy.

Why is this? It's because, by and large, we do not understand how suffering can heal us, draw us out of ourselves, and bring us closer to unitive love with God. Intense suffering is uncomfortable, which is indisputable. I've often squirmed and writhed inside as I've faced people's very raw and visible pain, but I know that being with another person in this agony is not only a gift to him or her, but is also a gift to me. I've never learned so much about life as when I have simply been with another person who has lived the Agony in Garden, the Scourging, the Crowning with Thorns, the Carrying of the Cross, and the Crucifixion.

Yet we know the world tells us otherwise: eschew suffering, because it is purely evil. Be comfortable or, even better, be *happy*. Seek the highest form of happiness that exists in this world, and all will be right in your soul. If we ponder this even for a millisecond, we realize how phony and incomplete this philosophy is, yet few of us challenge it, because, let's face it: suffering is hard.

The world convincingly displays happiness as the highest end to seek, and it is directly opposed to the evils and darkness of suffering and sorrow. In turn, we internalize our grief. We are left with unanswered questions. We are expected to wallow silently in our anger, to shed invisible tears when alone rather than in front of others. We are scorned and shunned if we risk the vulnerability of reaching out to another person in our distress.

Happiness is not the highest order for us to seek and strive for, because it is transitory and emotive. Joy supersedes the mere feeling of happiness, because it is rooted in the spirit of one's being rather than in the fickle feelings that flutter in the heart. Secularists posit that pleasure is the ultimate conduit of happiness, so whatever pleases us should be the primary means for capturing happiness in our lives. While the world entices us to cater to the sensory delights of our bodies, God challenges us to taming that fire so that we can know a deeper, more meaningful spiritual delight: joy.

Joy may, on occasion, include happiness, but it is not exclusive to such emotions. In fact, one may be in a state of joy and actually feel sorrowful. With this juxtaposition, we might be tempted toward happiness rather than joy, because we find the thought of sadness mingling with joy to be repugnant. Yet this is where the challenge becomes an opportunity for mastery: we choose joy, much as we choose love. The spiritual ecstasy that enraptured many saints is indeed available to us through the simplicity of joy. As a conscious act, we begin by praising God for who He is rather than what He has or hasn't done for us. Then we expand that prayer into gratitude for our blessings, and joy is often the fruit of such prayer. In this way, we may be in the depths of grief and our hearts stricken with anguish, yet our souls are elevated to a higher state of joy that floods us with the "peace that surpasses all understanding" (cf. Phil. 4:7).

Society's perspective on difficult and negative emotions has permeated the individuals with whom we dwell in community. As individuals, we have become incredibly unnerved with the subject of death, because it forces us to face our own mortality and revisit those enduring queries about the meaning of life and death, what we face *after* death. But the most feared question of all is what will happen when we face God and, ultimately, the truth—about ourselves and the way in which we have lived and loved.

So we do not contemplate these deep thoughts on a daily basis. We immerse ourselves in the monotony of laundry, dishes, groceries, errands, and extracurricular activities with kids, pets, or friends. We busy ourselves with our technology, playing games or music or keeping the television on as constant background noise. We are too exhausted at the end of a long day's work even remotely to desire facing the question of objective truth.

We force our consciences and our souls to become muted. We harden our hearts to those around us who reach out for a listening ear or a helping hand. We cannot bear our own burdens, so how can we possibly—and comfortably—assist someone else who is in the nadir of difficulty? Complacency with the status quo satisfies us for a time, but our hearts beg us to pay attention to the pain we suppress. And love begs us to step outside of societal mores and into the lives of others.

Humans long for companionship. We seek intimacy, but we often ignore the work and discipline that is required to constantly cultivate those relationships. Most of us desire more emotional and spiritual depth than what we currently receive. Most of us want those authentic encounters with others. We admire people who are real and honest, but we just can't bear to be among them.

Why not? Why can't we begin where other people dare not venture: *into the darkness, into the unknown?* Why don't we trust God enough to take His hand into ours and make the first step by practicing what we ourselves desire from others: listening to a person's stories of adversity, offering a hug or squeeze of the hand when someone cries in front of us, affirming that person when he or she apologizes for being too weepy, extending a prayer or knowing nod while he or she vents in anger?

It starts out as a taboo of society but can change with you and with me. We can first begin by recognizing how grief presents itself to us uniquely and then pray that we may be God's vessels of hope and strength to others who are in a place of despondency and hopelessness. We can recall what it felt like when we, too, were once dwelling in the land of darkness, and so we can be witnesses of the courage and serenity we have attained along our own voyage toward healing.

Healing begins when we acknowledge and affirm the reality of suffering and then permit ourselves to experience the difficult emotions that accompany our suffering and eventually allow it to transform our lives for some greater good rather than discarding and evading it. When others recognize our sincerity, they will understand the unspoken permission to share their own stories. That is how healing compounds. It begins with us but doesn't end there. It is the way in which we become God's hands and heart to a world that is infested with so much brokenness.

Healing cannot occur when we dwell in denial and seek only comfortable lives. Healing requires opening wounds and presenting them—in faith—to a God who perennially loves and desires to heal us in His mercy. Then we find our commissioning and go forth to live the spiritual and corporal works of mercy to people who are lost, broken, and wandering aimlessly without fully living their God-given charisms and gifts.

God doesn't operate in the comfort we seek; rather, He gently encourages us to step outside of what is known and desired into a realm of the unknown—mystery. It is in this mystery that God meets us, and we realize that He is mystery itself. In the unfamiliar places, we are stretched and formed, pruned and tried. It is where we face our ugliness and nothingness, where we are emptied and finally meet God with little to offer Him but our pain. While this feels horrific, it is actually the best gift we can present to God, because it is the only way He can fill us with every good thing—when our ego has been demolished.

The struggle of the human condition is a prerequisite for fullness of love. When we live in a manner that invites both tragedy and triumph, others will recognize our attempt at authenticity. People are attracted to genuineness, and yet so often they do not know how or where to begin living an unpretentious life themselves. Our witness to others by how we choose to live is a powerful testimony that invites them to follow suit in a way that is nonthreatening and approachable.

We perpetuate personal healing when we extend it to others, time and again. This is what will break the entrenched tendency to dodge the discussion and expression of suffering in our society. While this kind of metamorphosis doesn't usually happen in one day, we can be intentional with how we choose to respond to a world in need of the gifts we have to offer. If we take the time to pause long enough and ask God how we can effect change in someone's life today, He will most assuredly enlighten and direct us toward those who are in dire need of the hope that we have.

The need for this type of charity is far greater than the current supply of people actually living it, but you and I can opt to listen and respond to the movements of the Holy Spirit as He awakens our hearts to the cries of the poor and the sorrowful. We are not only God's hands and feet; we are also His heart, and He needs us to demonstrate His love to the most spiritually destitute among us.

The Healing Power of Laughter

Most of the time, it is customary to sniffle and occasionally dab one's eyes while wearing black to a funeral. People expect us always to feel sad or to cry after we have experienced any type of loss, but sometimes God sends levity at just the precise moment to elevate our spirits and heal our soul.

Laughter is considered psychologically healing while also producing physiological changes in our countenance and throughout our bodies.[13] Various parts of our brains are accessed when we laugh, particularly the frontal lobe and "sensory processing area

---

[13] Marshall Brain, "How Laughter Works," April 1, 2000, How Stuff Works, accessed November 19, 2015, http://science.howstuffworks.com/life/inside-the-mind/emotions/laughter.htm.

of the occipital lobe." The limbic system, composed of the amygdala, hippocampus, thalamus, and hypothalamus, stimulates our emotional responses. Perhaps not surprisingly, the hypothalamus is the location where laughter is processed in the brain.

Laughter, then, is highly integrated in our emotional responses to life circumstances. When we engage in a hearty belly laugh, the resulting bodily calm and catharsis is literally palpable. This validates the old adage "Laughter is the best medicine" when we both engage in and understand the biological origins of laughing.

Spiritually speaking, laughter can provide us with a chance to reframe our mournful perspective and recall that life is still worth living, even and especially in the midst of tragedy and pain. Smiling and laughing are the human attributes and expression of joy, which is the spiritual fruit of such behavior. With joyful mirth, our minds and bodies respond positively, and the paradox of emoting both sadness and happiness synchronously is actualized. Something seemingly so simple as a smile or a laugh lightens both our surroundings and our spirits. In these moments, we recall the complexities of life and death, and even death can illuminate more than just our interior life. God blesses us with more than one way to interject the recurring theme of light in the midst of such dark moments in our lives. When we focus on the light, the darkness dims and becomes tolerable and even preferable when we consider the importance of both light and darkness.

While grief is a complex spiritual occurrence, depression includes specific clinical criteria for diagnosis. Grief and depression include either the internalization or expression of negative emotions, which are shunned and discouraged in our modern society. Unfortunately this leads to denial and evasion of inevitable suffering and struggle. The human condition includes a tangible tension—progression and regression—in our interior lives, which is often based on our life experiences. When we risk opening the messy, hideous parts of ourselves that we'd rather conceal from others (and we do so in light of grace and for the sake of authentic relationship), we become God's instruments of change that tear down the invisible barricades that uphold our emotional façades. Life begins to transform us and others in this light, and God's mercy enters into those small openings in our hearts. We offer these to Him while we lament our losses, and we do so with great hope in what is to come.

2

Examples of Life Events
That Can Trigger Grief

It's not earth-shattering to say that there exist innumerable events in our lives that can propel us into grief. However, it wasn't until well into my adulthood that I could pinpoint my pain, as well as other people's, back to the origin of grief. It can be oversimplified, perhaps, but often the acknowledgment that one is experiencing grief can lend a slight relief. It often alleviates some of the agony by eliminating the unknown factor in why we are feeling and reacting the way are in a given moment.

This chapter will look at just a few possible experiences that can trigger grief. The short illustrations of each might help you recognize a similar experience in your own life that you can use as a point of reference for the remainder of this book.

Death

Death is the most reasonable place to begin when referencing grief, because it is the universal phenomenon we consider when the words *grief* and *mourning* are mentioned. Most of us grow up erroneously assuming that death is the only stimulus for launching one into a period of sadness and retrospection.

From Grief to Grace

Death is, of course, the one event that affects each of us—if not with someone we know personally, then with us. We all realize our mortality, and yet we don't often face its possible imminence—not until someone we know has died. Even then, the reality of our own life's end is often too much to bear, and so we forge ahead without a second thought, once our culture's rituals have ended (viewings, funerals, burials, and so forth).

Do we ponder our life's end? At times, during prayer, this thought can put into perspective the ways in which we utilize the brevity of time we have been allotted, how we have prioritized our relationships and whether we are truly living what we claim to believe as Catholics. This is not a morose preoccupation with death, but is a point for personal reflection and, often, growth in humility.

In pondering death, we can consider the greatness of the infinite God while admitting that we are finite creatures. In this way, we are filled with the fear of the Lord and may realize our desire to make each moment of our lives matter, so that our death—as well as our life—may be holy. There is a grace in being aware of our mortality from time to time, as it brings up questions posed in chapter 1: *What is our purpose on this earth? Where will we go after we die?* These are often the questions we put in the back of our minds as we go on with the busyness of business and daily living, yet they are pertinent to the existential understanding of humanity: our beginning and our end.

Experiencing death and the grief that follows varies for every one of us. In fact, grief may commence when we know someone has fallen ill or is in the stages of dying but has not yet passed on to eternity. Yet grief will most assuredly take on new dimensions once the person's soul has, in fact, left this earth. We will likely experience death differently with each person who has died. We may respond with anger or an embodiment of peace. We grieve more or less intensely. Sometimes we expect the level of grief that surfaces, but often we are astonished and bewildered when we do or do not cry, even when we want to be able to release that tension through tears.

Grief, like life and death, fluctuates and is often disordered and erratic. We must move with it instead of against it, forming no preconceived expectations for ourselves or others. It is helpful simply to be aware of our emotions and reactions, hand them over to God as an act of prayer, and learn from the suffering we encounter, as well as comfort those around us who mourn.

The first death that changed my entire perspective on suffering, life, death, and eternity was my grandfather's. Every one of us encounters these mysteries of human existence in a variety of ways, but each mystery we share contributes to our deeper understanding of who God is and how He truly loves us and wants us to be with Him forever.

Being present throughout my grandfather's senior years and the days preceding his death, as well as the day he died, made a profound and irrevocable impact on my life. Those few days I spent with my grandfather still linger heavily in my memory. They were—as most similar occasions are—bittersweet and yet filled with an odd tranquillity. At the time, I found this to be supremely bizarre, as every other death I had encountered left me feeling only restless and angry. But Grandpa's was different. We all knew where he was going—at worst, to Purgatory, and at best, to Heaven.

We never spoke about death, never used the word *death* in those final conversations. What was implied somehow spoke more boldly than if we had revisited the certainty and finality of death we all knew was approaching.

When my mother and I arrived at the nursing home, Grandpa could not breathe well. He was drifting in and out of consciousness, and during the lucid moments, he would panic and gasp for air. I sat by my grandpa, helpless and clueless as to how I should respond.

The Holy Spirit nudged me, and I acted on that prompting. I took Grandpa's hand—as I had only days before—and I squeezed it, clearly speaking in the ear closest to me, "Grandpa, it's me, Jeannie. Mom and I are here now, and we aren't going to leave you." Grandpa's eyelids fluttered, and he squeezed my hand.

It was the final earthly connection my grandpa and I would share.

Despite the darkness of death that hovered in the air, my heart was filled with the loftiness and grandeur of Heaven. It was what I saw that day: mercy, love, eternal rest. It was as if every theological lesson I had been taught and every truth that had been inscribed in my mind was now imprinted in my heart.

During his funeral, I was one of only a few people present who did not cry. I knew it was socially acceptable—and even expected—for people to cry during a funeral, but I could not muster even one tear. In fact, I was singing all the hymns with extraordinary exuberance, but I tried to be inconspicuous to those in surrounding pews. A slight smile remained on my lips, because, to me, the entire sanctuary was filled with a supernatural luminary that far exceeded our sorrows on earth.

Perhaps you have experienced a beautiful death that followed a beautiful life. Sharing someone's dying moments can be quite an honor, yet perhaps an unwelcome one. The gift of encountering a person at the most vulnerable time of his or her life can stir feelings of discomfort within us as we face the stark reality of our own mortality and of the impending loss of our loved one.

But this sharing is mutually beneficial, because our presence can be the consolation our loved one needs to persevere to the end, while we, too, can grow profoundly in our understanding of eternity through such an experience.

As mentioned in chapter 1, death is the most common life event that people consider when the word *grief* is mentioned. In fact, many people would wrongfully presume that it is the only life event that involves grief. What's important is to consider how we deal with death: Do we think of the afterlife now instead of waiting until we are facing our mortality because of a crisis?

There are three simple ways to manage death and the subsequent grief that lingers. First and most importantly, we need to ponder the condition of our souls on a daily basis, which can be done through a simple evening examen.[14] Typically this will draw us nearer to the sacrament of Reconciliation, which keeps our souls in a state of grace or at least allows us to see ourselves honestly and clearly so that we have frequent opportunities to correct our sins through Confession.

Secondly, we have a remarkable opportunity to walk with people in their journey of pain when someone they love passes into eternity. This is a rare and yet treasured gift to offer those who are grieving: the gift of your presence. Sit with them in

---

[14] My favorite type of examen is based on Ignatian spirituality, which includes five basic principles to follow at the end of each day: (1) Be aware of God's presence with you; (2) revisit your day with thanksgiving; (3) consider your feelings and acknowledge them without judgment; (4) select one part of your day and pray about it; (5) be grateful for being able to start over tomorrow. See "The Daily Examen," Ignatian Spirituality, accessed November 7, 2015, http://www.ignatianspirituality.com/ignatian-prayer/the-examen.

silence. Offer to pray with them. It will not be comfortable, so don't expect it to be. Instead, be at ease with the discomfort, and rest with the struggle the other person is experiencing. Intense emotions, especially negative ones, such as anger or fear, often result from death, but if you can rest in their expression of grief without judgment, you are well on the way to being a refuge for others in their time of suffering.

Thirdly and lastly, be an authentic witness of redemptive suffering to the people in your life. Only you will understand how this will unfold as you spend time in prayer and discernment, but most often it will spring from a place of deep delight and serenity in being who you are as a reflection of God. When we live a life that exemplifies the truth of human anguish through grappling with deep pain while searching to find meaning and joy within the struggle, others are subtly given permission to do the same. This is powerful and could eventually shift the societal paradigm from silencing our suffering to embracing and experiencing it fully.

Infertility, Miscarriage, and Abortion

Most of us unquestioningly assume when we are young that we will get married and have children—as many or as few as we want and when we want. We sometimes start making plans for the nursery and imagine where our newborn will sleep before we are even officially pregnant. We must come to terms with the fact that God is the author of life, just as He is the grantor of death, and sometimes He says no to our yes to the openness to having biological children.

Most of the time, we don't really want to accept this, do we? We want to be in control. We want God to conform to our will, our plans, our hopes and dreams. Our lives are centered on this age-old struggle between the human will and God's will for us. I had inadvertently adopted some of these beliefs, but it was during this time of waiting for our first child (and not knowing whether God would bless us with one) that the spiritual gift of fear of the Lord swelled in my heart.

Having children is always a gift and never a right for any couple. Our hearts are open, ready, and willing to welcome children, but sometimes that waiting is a preparation for the crosses we may eventually endure. It is God's gentle way of encouraging us to grow, bit by bit, and challenge our fears of the unknown factors that we all face every day.

Infertility is a type of grief about *what has never existed* rather than the loss of something or someone you already held and loved. In this way, infertility is set apart from other aspects of bereavement, and it is precisely why most people in our culture do not understand why those who suffer infertility grieve at all. If we never lost someone or something, how can a conspicuous void exist? Many infertile couples hear the empty platitudes from well-meaning people: "Don't worry; you're young. You'll have children someday. Why are you concerned about it?"

Even among other infertile couples, it may seem as if another person's experience with infertility somehow invalidates yours, depending on the length of time it takes to conceive a child. I was once told, "Well, at least it didn't take you *two years* to get pregnant, as it did for me." Upon reflection, I wondered, *Does it really matter how long it takes for someone to get pregnant?* If they experience infertility for six months or six years, it is still a cross.

Like infertility, miscarriage is often an unmentionable topic in our society. When we lose a child born to heaven instead of earth, we may hear people murmur, "Well, miscarriage is perfectly normal. I'm sure you'll be able to have another child someday." But the assumption that we can easily conceive and carry a child to full term with no complications is, in fact, an act of God. It is no less than a true miracle. Those of us who have experienced the pain of infertility and miscarriage understand this well. We recognize the fragility of human life and that the very Author of life is truly the one who ordains every little person's life in the world and out of it as well.

When we lose a baby in the early stages of pregnancy, it's very easy to dismiss as being "normal" or even to deny that we were pregnant in the first place. As most women know, we simply rationalize that we were just "late" without giving the possibility of miscarriage another thought or consideration. But every child we "lose," be it the child who was never born at all or the one who was born to Heaven, is still a precious and valuable member of our families.

And we must not neglect the parents who mourn the child they will never meet face-to-face in this life: the laugh they will never hear, the eyes that will never gaze into theirs, and the milestones they will never experience as a family.

Infertility and miscarriage are segues into the topic of abortion, because the societal ideologies that influence one area of reproduction often carry over into the others. Society tells us that children are a right rather than a gift. If a couple merely desires a child, then they most certainly have a right to that. We so easily accept this erroneous rationale without validating the grief that results from all the difficulties encircling the unique challenges of infertility, miscarriage, and abortion. This only compounds the suffering of those who are bereft over the loss of a child.

Although I have not personally experienced abortion, I know people who have. I have become close to women who have shared their stories with me and the guilt that erodes their emotions. Abortion scars everyone in society. None of us is exempt from its aftermath. Certainly an entire generation or two have already suffered the consequences of the "culture of death" and human-disposal mentalities.

Where are the mothers and fathers who have lost children to abortion in all of the madness? They are often forgotten and remain hidden in the hollows of invisible grief. Many, out of shame, do not dare speak of their choice to terminate their pregnancies, and most regret those decisions terribly. Even those men and women who proudly proclaim that they do not regret having had abortions have somehow not met that wound within their hearts quite yet.

How, then, do we respond to those who silently suffer from the effects of infertility, miscarriage, and abortion? Since the topic of reproduction is a sensitive one, it's best to wait for a person to open the topic of discussion with you. When someone does, ask the Holy Spirit for wisdom in how to respond. Mutual trust is crucial when someone feels comfortable enough to share this silent grief with another person.

Another option for promoting infertility and miscarriage awareness is by participating in or starting a diocesan or parish ministry that includes group sessions in which participants can share their stories in a safe environment. On occasion, parishes offer a special Mass for parents who have lost their babies to miscarriage, but by and large, the Church can grow tremendously in an effort of outreach to these families who may not know how or where to turn when they face the pain of infertility and miscarriage.

The grief resulting from abortion very much mirrors that of Post-Traumatic Stress Disorder: flashbacks, recurring nightmares, anxiety, and insomnia.[15] Those of us who befriend the mothers and fathers of aborted children should approach them gingerly and with tenderness. We must listen to their stories, however difficult they may be to hear, and receive them in great love.

Because the aftermath of reproductive loss is always a deep-seated heartache that has been silenced somewhere in their lives, people afflicted with infertility, miscarriage, or abortion need someone to assist them spiritually in opening that wound so that it can be healed. The beginning of that healing can occur through the loving encounter of your relationship with that person, and if you are that person, start sharing your story, and others will know that they are not alone in their grief.

Broken Relationships and Divorce

Whether or not we have personally been affected by divorce, we probably know multitudinous people who are divorced or whose parents are divorced. Divorce and broken relationships can trigger grief, and the longer we have shared our life with a person, the more grievous the wound when that relationship is broken. It is as if a part of us, our very identity, is stripped from us. We are left feeling like half a person, not knowing who we are without the other. It is a strange phenomenon to navigate the confusion of starting over without the one person with whom we have become comfortable and so accustomed to living, to whom we have become so familiar and whom we have grown to love through mutual commitment.

---

[15] For a full list of these symptoms, visit the Mayo Clinic's article on Post-traumatic Stress Disorder at http://www.mayoclinic.org/diseases-conditions/post-traumatic-stress-disorder/basics/symptoms/con-20022540.

Whereas we are expected to mourn a spouse who has died, when divorce or a broken relationship occurs, the expectation is to rejoice at the new opportunities that await us. We are told simply to "find someone else" and "move on." What are we to make of the actuality that our lives have been permanently altered? Some very real and deep-seated wounds may result from this ultimate form of betrayal. How can we learn to trust another person again?

One acquaintance offered an additional insight into divorce that I had never considered: unlike death, grief due to divorce *lacks rituals*. When a person dies, we receive closure through the burial rites and symbols associated with it. But what symbols exist for closure with an ex-spouse? There are none, and for a person who longs for closure when a marriage has ended, to what does he or she turn?

The wound of betrayal takes many, many years to heal. The longer the marriage, the deeper the wound may be. Some say that divorce was a healing experience for them and that they simply made a mistake in selecting a life partner, while others say they did not want the divorce and felt ostracized by the mutual friends they and their ex-spouse shared. Either way, we must consider the fragments that are left behind when divorce occurs.

Even in unions that did not include children, the couple presumably gave everything to each other: deepest thoughts, most vulnerable fears and feelings, and physical intimacy. They shared bizarre quirks, foibles, and idiosyncrasies with each other that perhaps not even their parents or closest friends could comprehend well. Sharing a life with someone entails far more than simply sharing a house or a bed or even an occasional meal. It is more than sharing children. It necessarily involves self-sacrifice.

Many people do not enter marriages that are entirely self-sacrificial. In fact, doing so may be more the exception than the rule. Even so, the marriage bond necessarily unites a couple in a profound, irrevocable manner—imperceptible perhaps, unfulfilled perhaps, but when this bond is broken, we cannot imagine the wound of grief that creeps in the heart. It seems to be one that is most grievous and complex. Divorce is like a phantom or shadow that always hovers and cannot be eradicated from one's life.

When a person dies, we enter a period of expected mourning. When we grieve a child who never existed or one lost to miscarriage or abortion, we add another layer of complexity to that grief due to the absence of the child's body for closure. The dimension is no longer blatantly obvious. It then becomes cloudy and obscured in a murky fluctuation between societal standards and confronting our own reality. It seems something similar would ensue as a result of divorce—the nebulous domain of not actually having lost a person to the finality of death, but rather losing a relationship that exists in a new, different form.

Many divorced individuals no longer feel as if they are welcome in social circles within the Church, because they have become the anomalies while their married friends still share so much in common with each other. This aspect of their grief may build loneliness that can lead to isolation if no one notices or reaches out to befriend them.

If you are divorced, tell your friends if you are lonely and would like to be included in social activities. If you know someone who is newly divorced, invite that person over for a family dinner or a holiday gathering. Keep asking even if the person initially declines. For those who are divorced, it helps to know to whom they can turn when they are ready.

Divorce ministries are also needed in our churches, and divorce support groups are already blossoming in some parishes. Divorcées and divorced men may find camaraderie when they are considered extended family members and continue to be invited to parish events. The key to understanding grief in any of its forms is to simply listen to the one who is aggrieved. Listen and be with that person. Sometimes this is enough (or more than enough) for him or her to feel incredibly loved, not only by you but also by God. Remember that you are God's vessel of charity, and often this means reaching out to those who aren't sure how to ask for help.

Addiction

I was twelve years old when I witnessed the decline of a beloved relative due to her addiction to crack cocaine. I don't recall if I asked my parents bluntly or if they simply told me about her drug addiction, but the truth was revealed to me over time. In high school, this was the only testimony I had known firsthand of this type of tragedy. My cousin died in her early forties from heart failure and what was speculated to be a result of those hard years of drug abuse.

Although this was my first memory of addiction, its horrors unraveled in my life as an adult. My younger brother became adept at hiding alcohol during family gatherings, and I was truly oblivious to his inebriation. When I became privy to his alcoholism and addiction, I was soon enveloped in anger. Flashbacks of many years and several bizarre get-togethers in which my brother was present suddenly came to the fore. I knew in retrospect that things were out of sync with him, and I was angry at myself for not having noticed how badly he had spiraled into alcoholism.

From Grief to Grace

Sudden tragedies related to senseless and irresponsible decisions, to this day, leave me speechless and incredibly enraged. In such situations, I have dealt with grief on two levels: with the loss of these loved ones' lives and with the addictions that stole them from me long before their deaths. I have tried, but I cannot reconcile how the consequences of their choices were so bitter, so final. It has always seemed such a waste of young lives and vibrant—albeit hurting—souls to succumb to the darkness of addiction.

Addiction takes many forms besides illicit substance abuse: gambling, sex, pornography, shopping, and overeating are among the more common associations of addiction. In all cases, the brain is triggered in a compulsory manner to need the substance or the act that will temporarily relieve the person of the craving. Anxiety can be directly related to this craving. So addiction is both biological and psychological. It is a true disease, one that has no universal, identifiable cure.

Most of us who are plagued with the grief of addiction at some point believe we have caused it in some way or that the addict can simply will himself to stop. If that doesn't work, perhaps we can will the addict to stop—by controlling what he does, by dumping out alcohol or controlling his finances—and we obsess over how we can force him to quit his habit.

The truth is we are perpetuating the madness of addiction when we enter into the insanity of futilely trying to control behaviors. Perhaps this is a manifestation of our grief: that we recognize that the nightmarish situations surrounding the disease are absolutely out of our grasp, but it soothes our sense of helplessness to regain some sense of jurisdiction over the chaos. We find ourselves in the midst of this chaos, and we grasp for straws, often engaging in completely irrational behavior that often mimics the addict's.

The grief associated with addiction is in watching a person waste away and decay from the inside out. Having known many people before an addiction took over their lives, I have seen the healthy version of them as well as the sick version. It's as if I am observing an invisible cancer consume a very beautiful soul. You see, people who suffer from various addictions are *good people*. They are often very loving and amicable, talented and brilliant. But they have not learned to cope with suffering in a healthy manner, and once they begin riding that slippery slope, it's often difficult to reverse.

What is most humbling is accepting that we are no different from the addict. If we were ever to choose to use an illicit substance or engage in destructive (and possibly immoral) behavior, we would most likely become an addict. Addiction is a family disease and tends to have a genetic correlation, but this is also true because of the physiological transformation that occurs in the pleasure center of the brain when we engage an addiction.

Addicts attempt to dull an ache in their hearts and souls. Addiction serves as a mask to intense trauma that is difficult for the person to alleviate otherwise. We all know that grief can be absolutely unbearable and overwhelming at times. But what about the person whose grief has become complicated, in that it is a daily source of pain that only increases with the passing of time? Some people are tormented in ways we cannot fathom, and once they are introduced to a fleeting opportunity at appeasing that excruciating pain, it is as if a balm has softened the edges of their pain—for a time.

Of course, the pain resumes, often more exacerbating than before. So the addict continues to numb that pain in the only way he knows can instantly alleviate the emotional brokenness in him. To him, it is worth the temporary fix for a moment's relief, even though many addicts are intelligent and fully cognizant of the consequences of their choices.

The day I learned to embrace my brother (and my deceased loved ones who had died as a result of prolonged drug abuse) was the day I welcomed serenity into my life. It was cathartic: a release and a relief to be rid of the oppression that had been weighing me down emotionally for so many years.

In this newfound peace, we can become comfortable with people who are in the thick of extremely intense and horrifying suffering. Part of our attempt at control is to appease our own discomfort at their visible anguish. When we let go not only of our efforts to control (which are fruitless anyway) but also of the other person's suffering, a certain level of emotional maturity develops in us. We become not only capable of being with people in the midst of severe agony (mostly emotional and psychological in nature), but we also want to *be with them*.

In becoming comfortable with ourselves, we become at ease with the addict. And somehow we are able to reconcile his unresolved struggles with our own discomfort with suffering. The fruit of peace carries the grace of charity on its wings. It is a genuine love for the addict that draws us to be with him in his suffering.

Twelve-step programs are incredibly insightful when you know and love someone who is suffering from any type of addiction, because the program facilitates inner healing for you rather than for the addict. This is so liberating to begin the world of self-awareness rather than focusing on the often unhealthy, codependent attempt to control the addict. Even if no one else changes, we must remember to exercise our free will. We must relish that gift and grace, always choosing to love the addict where he is without desiring to alter him.

It's also helpful to learn how to set appropriate emotional (and perhaps literal) boundaries with the addicts we know and love. In the cloud of their brokenness, they are often boundary-less and unaware of how their behavior may provoke our grief. Some experts have called this "tough love," but essentially setting boundaries is something you can determine only through prayer and possibly counseling. For one person, the boundary might be no communication with the addict under any circumstances, while another person may have undisrupted contact but refuse to provide housing or money.

The grief of addiction is twofold, because both the addict and the ones who love the addict lament over what once was and what could be. Despite the destruction of drugs and alcohol to the body and mind, many addicts remain oblivious or unscathed by this reality and yet persistently exist in a state of anesthetized woundedness, which distresses their family and friends. Love from a distance can often assuage the wounds of the addict's loved ones, at least for a time, while concurrently offering new insight into healthy detachment from the disease of addiction.

Mental Illness and Chronic Diseases

The characteristics of mental illnesses and chronic diseases can overlap. For one, people who suffer from prolonged psychological diagnoses—particularly ones that have no cure—walk a path similar to that of those who struggle with a long-term heart condition, asthma, allergies, diabetes, autoimmunity, and other comparable illnesses. The difference is that psychological diagnoses are sometimes easy to overlook, because many people walking among us who battle them silently appear typical and may blend in with the rest of society. It is unfortunate that our culture presents mental illness in frightening depictions of violence and volatility. In reality, most people who have been diagnosed with major depressive disorder, for example, are not harmful or terrorizing.

Purely physiological diagnoses, such as diabetes or congestive heart failure, are much more acceptable to most of us than mental illness. When physical manifestations of a disease are visible, we tend to sympathize with the sufferer. But it is much more complicated to do so with those afflicted with mental distress and emotional struggles, especially if we have not experienced anything comparable in our own lives.

It is understandable why the stigma of mental illness lingers in this day and age among those who are not learned in physiological psychology. Most psychological diagnoses (with the exception of personality disorders) originate in the neurotransmitter substances and/or structure of the brain. For example, people who struggle with obsessive-compulsive disorder have lower levels of serotonin in their brains than do their typical peers. Conversely, those with schizophrenia show much higher levels of dopamine in their brains than do their typical counterparts.

I chose the field of psychology primarily out of a desire to understand human thinking and behavior. During the latter part of my childhood and throughout my adolescence, I lived with active mental illnesses, and I could not make sense of how and why they occurred. I was frightened at the prospect that I, too, might one day become afflicted with mental illness due to genetic predisposition, and I languished with my younger brother as I watched him scuffle with everyday life.

Although the exact time frame is unclear in my memory, I do recall that life took a gradual turn for our family when my brother manifested bizarre behaviors. He would ask a question of one of us, then repeat it twice, wait for the answer, and repeat the answer to himself twice. At first, my parents and I made light of this strange game, but it became more obvious that my brother was suffering anxiety that increased as the days passed.

More unusual patterns evolved, in which my brother would organize his collections of sports jerseys and hats, none of which he wore and all of which he displayed with museum-quality perfection in his bedroom. If anything touched them, it caused my brother extreme anxiety.

My parents investigated potential counselors and happened upon a clinic that specialized in obsessive-compulsive disorder (OCD). Call it serendipity or divine providence, but it was a huge relief to my parents when they discussed my brother's behavior with the psychologist who founded this clinic. After the intake was complete, my brother was diagnosed with OCD. Thus began the long road to recovery, not just for my brother but also for the entire family.

When my brother hit puberty, another level of explosiveness emerged. His rage and fury would flare up at my mother and me seemingly out of nowhere. There were times when my parents were not home that I would run into my bedroom, lock the door, and sob because my brother was so angry that I was convinced he was going to hurt me. Sometimes he did threaten me. He chased me with a baseball bat, a stick, a shovel—whatever he could find at the time. I had to hold my door shut with my study chair and push against his force with all my strength. I didn't relent until I was certain he had given up.

I pined for God's healing touch in our family and prayed ceaselessly for a reprieve from the intensity and uncertainty of my brother's psychological hardships. It was horrendous to watch him sobbing in his bedroom when he believed no one else was home. On one occasion, I had come home from school early and was walking upstairs to complete my homework. As I passed my brother's room, his door was cracked open, and I quietly peered in. I witnessed him delicately caressing the photographs in an old album when we were children, and in between sobs, he would whimper, "God, why? When will this end?"

I felt as if my heart would rip into shreds. Part of me wanted to rush in and hold my brother, to cry with him, and to share his moment of suffering. But the greater part of me was terrified of his reaction, not knowing whether he would welcome or rebuff my presence. Because the wound of his precarious behavior toward me was still fresh, I chose to walk away and cry in the solitude of my bedroom.

I spoke to God as I did to my closest friends. Although I couldn't see Him, I envisioned Him sitting on the loveseat next to my bed, listening intently and without concern for time. I always knew God existed outside of time, so it was effortless for me to drone on and on about the trivialities of my life as well as the tragedies. Journaling without censorship became an anticipated ritual that developed into healing therapy. I did not have to conform to social expectations or put on my daily pretense in front of classmates and teachers or coworkers and friends.

This liberation can be therapeutic. We may feel the release of the tension in our bodies when we write and speak to God. In turn, our hearts develop a longing to know, love, and serve God more and more. I begged Him to lead me to my calling so that I could somehow make sense of the interminable pain that was afflicting my entire family, because I wanted someday to make a positive impact on families who were experiencing similar struggles.

Walking with someone who has a psychological diagnosis can be tentative depending on the severity of the diagnosis. Because the human brain is unpredictable, despite neuropsychological advances, it's difficult to know how to approach someone who is exhibiting patterns of behavior that may seem out of character for him or her.

We can begin by educating ourselves about the illness itself, which erases the fears associated with what is unknown. Once we understand the etiology of the disease, we are more apt to be patient with outbursts, irrational thinking, and depressive or manic episodes. Although it's problematic to love some people with psychological diagnoses, it can—and must—be done, because they may feel trapped and isolated in their minds, not knowing if anyone truly understands them.

So simply love the one whom you may not fully understand. Set the boundaries that make you feel safe when you are with that person, but love him or her nonetheless. This requires introspection, prayer, and selfless acts of kindness and forgiveness. Love may not change your loved one or situation, but it will change your heart, and that is where the real transformation begins.

In every aspect of personal loss, there exist both the interior toil and the ultimate tenacity. Each loss necessitates change in our lives. We come to a crossroads, at which we can elect to grow in the midst of the uncertainty or to succumb to it and never discover the inner strength that increases as we surge forward. Opting to enter into unfamiliar and frightening territory invites risk of emotional vulnerability.

We are often overcome with a paralyzing fear before consciously taking that step toward change. We know that every loss invites a new beginning in our lives, yet we must embrace the metamorphosis before the ultimate glory emerges. This is the rhythmic tension of grief: the darkness of loss followed by the invitation to something new. Entering into our wounds with God requires a substantial leap of faith and incredible trust. We are then able to view the promise of spiritual healing without the certainty of how or when it will come to be—only that it will happen.

Grief takes on varying colors depending on the situation and person experiencing it. Part of this is due to our emotional and spiritual maturity, level of stress, health condition, and ability to cope with daily life generally. Another part is the gravity of the loss. To journey through grief, we must remember two things: to be kind and gracious through the difficult days and moments of joy and intentionally to seek the lost and lonely, hurting and wounded people who are suffering and desperately long to be loved through their losses.

Hope is often our solitary friend in the midst of darkness. It is the virtue that carries us when we have no utterances to God left within us, when we have become bone-weary, and when our crosses become so heavy that the darkness engulfs us. It is then that we take on the yoke of Jesus, who promises us that His burden is easy and light. Hope is concurrent with faith, for both require an element of accepting something contrary to human reasoning. Both hope and faith draw us to some-thing—Someone—beyond ourselves, so that we are capable of noticing the goodness that continues while we wrestle with our emotions.

Think of the rose in winter. Roses do not ordinarily bloom in winter, but our Lady has become my "Winter Rose." This is not merely because of the incredible story of St. Juan Diego unveil-ing a mass of roses when he opened his cloak to the bishop, but it is because winter is reminiscent of grief. It seems endless, as if nothing will ever be vibrant again. There is no color—only gray and the black of long, dark nights. The agony of winter's silence can be maddening, much like the torment of the wound of grief that seems to endure far past its initial impact.

Our Lady, our Winter Rose, is our oasis when the winter of grief tarries without end in sight. She refreshes us with the fragrance of hope: the ardor of love in the rose's rich, crimson hue and its subtle-but-sweet smell that raises our hearts to a place of supernatural elation. We are carried to God by the presence of our Lady when our hearts are rendered empty and hollow. When we are near despair, she lifts us to Him, and His divine grace envelops us until the storms of grief pass. When the clouds of darkness are lifted, the sweetness of life remains. When we choose to enter into our grief, we choose life. We choose the hidden gift that awaits us on the other side of darkness.

May we cleave to our Lady when the layers of grief are peeling away, bit by bit, and we have lost a sense of normalcy and purpose in the midst of our trials. She will lift us and carry us to the arms of Jesus, where we can rest for a time and simply be cherished by our Beloved.

Despite the type of situation that triggers grief, the important point is to begin recognizing how we respond to tragedy. We must become sensitized to our cognitive, emotive, and visceral reactions when our lives hit turning points, when crises overwhelm us, or when an unforeseen loss leaves us empty and mystified. Grief can grip us at any time, in any way, for any reason. It's best to prepare ourselves through self-examination and prayer so that we can tackle grief with a renewed sense of hope and resilience.

The great spiritual writer Thomas à Kempis offers us a final thought that can fortify our resolve to persevere through every suffering. We remain resolute to our faith, because God's promises are ever present and unfailing. Earth is not our final destination, so all our trials are temporary:

> Let not your labors which you have undertaken for my sake crush you, neither let tribulations from whatever source, cast you down, but in every occurrence let My promise strengthen and console you. I am sufficient in recompense to you beyond all bounds and measures. It is not long you have to labor here, nor will you always be oppressed with sorrows. Wait a little while and you shall see a speedy end to suffering.[16]

---

[16] Thomas à Kempis, *The Imitation of Christ* (Mineola, NY: Dover Publications, 2003), bk. 3, chap. 47.

3

The Grace of Redemptive Suffering

"Offer it up" became a cliché my mother used to direct my brother's and my thoughts from ourselves to the Cross. Although I hated hearing it ad nauseam, over time I learned its value and meaning. When I asked where my mom heard such a phrase, she would shrug and simply respond, "Every Catholic grows up hearing 'offer it up.' " There was seemingly never an origin for the phrase, only a passing of the tradition from the proverbial school nun to the common Catholic household.

Because I always heard the adage as a barking command rather than accompanied by an elaboration, I grew to resent it. I often said "offer it up" in mocking unison with my mom as I anticipated the moments when she would remind me: while raking the leaves for three hours, shoveling the driveway in freezing temperatures, poring over laborious and insipid homework, or completing household chores. This wasn't my mother's fault, of course, but rather it became an idiom void of explanation. It rang hollow on my ears and, more importantly, in my heart.

When suffering transforms from the menial drudgery of everyday chores to a chronic constant in our everyday life, we begin to recognize the value of keeping silent instead of grousing about trivialities. Greater burdens become more evident, and we are ashamed at our puerile grumblings.

After many years of hearing my mother's voice speak in frustration, "Offer it up," I finally adopted the instruction. It was no longer necessary to hear those words directed at me from an outside source. A time came when I heard the words interiorly, and I knew as I looked at Jesus on the crucifix in our living room that there was much I needed to learn about life, suffering, and death.

Quietly surrendering our sufferings contradicts our concupiscence, so we learn to pray for the grace to acquiesce to God's will. We can imagine that every time we silently accept a humiliation or complete an onerous task, it is done as a prayer for a lonely soul in Purgatory or for a family member or friend who is struggling inexorably. After a while, we begin to offer things up daily out of love rather than obligation or guilt. We learn that suffering and love are synonymous in nearly every way—at the very least, they are inextricably intertwined.

One way we can actively participate in offering up our grievances to God is through meditation on the Passion of Jesus through the Stations of the Cross and Sorrowful Mysteries of the Rosary,[17] not only during Lent, but on every Friday throughout the year. This can completely morph our understanding of what it means to suffer without complaint or restraint. This is not to say that we must enjoy suffering or ask God for more trials, but when trials inevitably appear in our lives, we present to God in prayer our initial resistance to accepting them. Our hearts may be filled with anguish not often tempered by love, but rather paralyzed in fear. Even if our lamentations are not spoken aloud, we certainly bring our share of gripes to God in prayer. We know

---

[17] See Appendix B.

The Grace of Redemptive Suffering

He asks us to carry our crosses, but we still want an easy life, free of the constant stream of frustrations and strife. The Cross draws us out of our whining and petty egocentrism into the eternal realm of solidarity. The concept of solidarity, then, summons us to suffer with and for the sake of God's kingdom on earth. Although it's valuable and even necessary to validate our uneasy feelings about carrying our crosses, it's more critical to subjugate ourselves to Jesus, even if it takes thousands of attempts in our lifetime to finally reach a place of true surrender. Perseverance is the key to overcoming our flesh, the devil, and the world—all of which tell us to seek comfort and pleasure rather than endure tribulations.

It becomes clearer to us, however, that if we are to fulfill our true call as Catholic Christians, we cannot live a comfortable life of luxury and concurrently grow in union with Jesus. At some point, we reach a crossroads at which we are faced with a decision: do as we please and be moderately "happy" in this life or walk with Jesus on the road to Calvary. We know walking with Jesus will not be a carefree path to traverse. We also realize it will be replete with thorns and tears, but we want to be with Him and please Him much more than we want the life that the world offers us.

Redemptive suffering is a concept foreign to most in our modern society. The world tells us in ways both subtle and blatant that happiness is achieved only through the acquisition of wealth, a lifestyle of materialism, and noteworthy achievements that lead to power or renown (or both). To embrace the gift of redemptive suffering fully requires a direct contradiction to what secularism dangles in front of us. Our modern world thrives on superficialities and frivolities, but our souls pine for far more than what the world can offer.

From Grief to Grace

Father Paul Duffner defines redemptive suffering in this way: "Christ gave to all suffering experienced in the members of His Mystical Body a redeeming power when [it is] accepted and offered up in union with His Passion.... By accepting willingly and without complaint the little inconveniences, irritations, frustrations, delays, setbacks, etc. which God in His Providence allows to come our way, we can pay in part the debt that we, or others, have incurred by our sins."[18] Although redemptive suffering is not an indulgence or automatic absolution for sin, it is a means by which we can wholeheartedly participate in Christ's Paschal Mystery so that our afflictions are not wasted but are directed to Heaven as a supplication for grace to intervene. In this way, our suffering compensates for the lack in the Body of the Church; therefore, redemptive suffering means that what we suffer fulfills the mission of the Church (see Col. 1:24). Essentially suffering is the means by which we can win souls for Heaven.

Naturally, redemptive suffering is also contrary to our fallen human nature. We are inherently conditioned to recoil at physical pain or emotional torment, yet the grace bestowed on us through the anointing at our Baptism and Confirmation is renewed time and again so that the "Spirit may overcome" our flesh (cf. Matt. 26:41). We are strengthened and given spiritual nourishment each time we receive Jesus in the sacrament of the Eucharist, and, every time we falter, we can experience God's mercy through the sacrament of Reconciliation. God knows the limitations of our humanity, but He has not left us orphaned.

[18] Father Paul A. Duffner, O.P., "Redemptive Suffering," *The Rosary Light and Life* 49, no. 2 (March–April 1996), accessed February 2, 2016, http://www.rosary-center.org/ll49n2.htm.

Our assent to redemptive suffering will drastically aid us in healing and recovering from both acute and chronic grief in our lives. When we stop running from God's invitation to open our hearts ever wider to the magnificent chasm of His love and mercy, we will discover peace infiltrating our entire being. Resistance to inexorable tribulations only exacerbates our grief. We may discover that we are thrust into a darker place than ever before, or perhaps the pain worsens or lingers a bit longer.

Embracing our cross is the essence of navigating grief. It is precisely the conscious act of entering into our wounds and permitting God to enter into our wounds that leads us to ultimate healing, peace, and joy. This chapter hones in on several aspects of redemptive suffering, based on a particular saint's or theological writer's perspective. We can learn much from their lives and come to understand better these gems of truth. They include recognizing the difference between holy and unholy darkness, understanding how holy indifference, abandonment to Divine Providence, and confidence in God's timing and humility all play integral roles in our navigation of grief.

There are six spiritual principles that can assist us on this journey of navigating our grief. The first principle is humility, which is the basis of all other virtues and interior growth. The second principle is abandonment to Divine Providence, the third holy indifference, the fourth the dark night of the soul, the fifth confidence in God's timing, and the final principle is the wound of the heart.

Where do these ideologies become adorned in our hearts? In the desert. The desert is a metaphor for the place in our interior life where we confront our nothingness and emptiness. It is a harsh but necessary discipline and formation, because we are rid of everything that has provided us with answers. The desert empties us, depletes us, and tries us through its winds and endless chilling nights. We are alone, too, to tread the sands and brave the heat in this remote location. Retreating to this desert place in our souls is where we find solitude and encounter Jesus.

Consider Moses' conversion that occurred when he thrust himself deep into the aridity of the unknown region beyond the Egyptian palace where he grew up as prince. He left everything behind him, including what he believed to be his very identity. Yet this wandering prompted reflection, and his journey soon became rhythmic, sensible, and clear. He found his mission in the desert (see Exod. 2ff.).

Jesus, too, withdrew to the desert for forty days (see Matt. 4:1–11), where He was tempted by the devil to pleasure, power, and pride. Those of us experiencing any sort of loss may be tempted to similar sins: pleasure in running from our pain instead of embracing it; power so that we can restore our sense of control rather than recognizing the gift of our weakness and emptiness; and pride in turning from God rather than toward Him in our misery. Jesus confronted Satan boldly, however, which sets a clear example for us when we are tempted to abandon God in our own desert journey. Instead of capitulating to the ease of sin, we can rebuke evil in the midst of our soul's austerity. The soul aches for God in the desert and always finds Him there.

To comprehend redemptive suffering fully, we must also explore God's perfect will (sometimes called positive, active, or ordained) versus His permissive (or passive) will.[19] God's perfect

---

[19] See Emily Stimpson, "Discerning God's Positive and Permissive Will," *Our Sunday Visitor Newsweekly*, June 13, 2012, accessed November 16, 2015, https://www.osv.com/OSVNewsweekly/

will is such that, because He is good, He wills only what is good and holy. Obviously He still allows tragedy to strike, disasters to destroy, and evil to flourish. The latter is His permissive will, which is more often than not the source of controversy in the argument that God is entirely benevolent. If God didn't permit these things to happen, quite simply, they wouldn't occur. But how can we wrap our minds around that truth and still maintain that God always wills our good?

Although "God did not make death" (see Wisd. 1:13), suffering and death are still very much a part of human existence. We can deduce this fact in part due to the nature of free will and its importance in our sanctification and also the consequences of our concupiscence. Sin and death can be synonymous to the spiritual thinker, so we know that neither is an aspect of God's perfect will, only His permissive will to bring about a greater good.

God's perfect will is what He wants: unity, peace, love, every soul to spend eternity with Him, and so forth. His permissive will is what He allows: storms and strife, diseases and death. In the beginning, every person was destined to be perfectly united with Him, but after the Fall of man and Original Sin, our souls were permanently severed from Heaven (until Jesus redeemed us, of course). Free will plays a huge act in the divine drama, but without it we would be as puppets manipulated by a puppeteer. Instead, God wants us to choose freely to follow Him.

God's permissive will is precisely where redemptive suffering fits into our understanding of how and why grief can become spiritually restorative for us. God didn't initially want suffering to exist, but once it did—through His permission—He wished

ByIssue/Article/TabId/735/ArtMID/13636/ArticleID/2585/
Discerning-Gods-positive-and-permissive-will.aspx.

it to be a channel of redemption and an opportunity for us to draw nearer to Him in and through love. We choose to love God when we aspire to suffer what God permits. In this, we unite our hearts with His.

First Spiritual Principle: Humility of Heart

In his spiritual classic *Humility of Heart*, Father Cajetan Mary de Bergamo tells us, "As all the troubles of this world are ordained by God and yours are sent to you by Him especially to humble your pride ... the best means to oblige God to deliver us from our troubles is to humble ourselves.... God sends adversity to you to humble you, and He humbles you so that from this humiliation you may learn humility."[20]

The foundation of interior formation when we are navigating grief is the virtue of humility, because its focus is on God and away from self. When we are grieving, we tend to be more self-focused, because pain is more egocentric rather than Christocentric. Humility, then, is essential for our formation toward healing, beginning with our desire for God to propagate it in our lives. Humility is typically acquired through acts of humiliation, which, of course, oppose our inclination to pride. When we grieve, humiliation may appear in the form of unexpected weeping to a compassionate stranger or permitting a neighbor to clean our house when we are emotionally drained and physically exhausted.

Pride is a vice with which we all battle. The root of *all sin* is pride, but nearly every manifestation of pride somehow rears

---

[20] This quotation and all others in this section are excerpted from Father de Bergamo's spiritual gem *Humility of Heart*, which was translated into English by Herbert Cardinal Vaughn, Archbishop of Westminster, England, in 1903.

its ugly head in our lives on a daily basis. What is humility, and what is it not? In reflecting upon what humility is not, we are better able to form a clearer concept of pride's nemesis. One thesis clearly woven throughout Father de Bergamo's *Humility of Heart* is that, when one believes one is humble, that very belief is actually a form of pride. And pride makes its appearance in our hearts and behaviors in ways both understated and blatant.

A proud individual thinks of and speaks of himself often and ostentatiously. He seeks accolades, affirmation, honor, status, and privilege. In contrast, a humble person seeks to be hidden and invisible. Not only is he content to be unknown, but he also prefers to be unacknowledged and even disavowed. To the humble person, scourges are sweet, especially wounds from God. But all acts of mortification are welcomed with gratitude, as the humble one is keenly aware of the benefits of these acts upon his soul. He gains eternal merit when he is rejected, scorned, abased, and despised. He knows this, and this is how wisdom and humility are interconnected.

A proud individual can be likened to a fool, because he is concerned only with what is external. He keeps up appearances and converses with people of influence in order to gain ground in his personal ambitions. He lacks wisdom, because he lacks depth of character.

A humble person, however, longs to remain small and as nothing in the secular sense. He is sincere and authentic, seeking to deepen his relationships with God and others. He values emotional and spiritual transparency over superficial facades. He desires to love others rather than to use them, knowing that love requires him to die to himself.

One who is humble walks the long and dusty road, riddled with thorns and rocks. His life — every aspect of it — seems difficult to others but is actually quite easy and desirable to him. The proud man, however, pursues the road to perdition, which is disguised as a pleasurable path adorned with riches and sensory delights.

Humility requires a spiritual nakedness, an openness and purposeful exposure of heart that is visible to both God and others. One who is humble prefers to showcase the truth through his failures without dwelling on them too long, which is false humility.

Such transparency is often another act of humiliation, because the vulnerability we expose to God in our emptiness and spiritual nakedness is frightening. We jeopardize losing everything we are; we risk rejection from the One who made us; and we risk the indispensable intimacy that self-knowledge provides our souls. Humility, then, involves honesty—with oneself, with others, and with God.

A humble person never plays the role of victim and does not feel comfortable when speaking of or focusing on himself, for he would much rather think of and glorify God. Yet he is comfortable with his humanity and embraces it with appreciation, for his concupiscence keeps him dependent on God alone.

The humble one is simple and poor in spirit. Thus, he has a pure heart. He knows that discipline is necessary to kill the remnant pride in him, and so he is relieved by intense purgation and privations actively or permissively willed by God. He also hides them, for he knows that displaying his state of struggle would attract attention and perhaps sympathy or even admiration from others. His holiness is kept secret, known only to God. Even when dying, he admits his sinfulness, although his sins are few.

Pride and humility are not always clearly differentiated. Consider the religiosity of the Pharisees in Scripture. Jesus often points to the Pharisees' behavior as examples of pride, rather than of humility (see Matt. 6:1–8). We may often observe pious behavior and presume a person is holy based on these exterior acts. On the contrary, we may meet people who are unkempt, uncouth, and otherwise socially inappropriate and assume they are far from Heaven. It is quite possible, however, that the truth is incompatible to our beliefs in both circumstances. That is why Jesus seeks humility *of heart*. Our actions must correspond with our interior motives. Father de Bergamo puts it succinctly: "Hidden acts of humility are safer than exterior ones." It's best to err on the side of caution and secretly accept the moments of humiliation that severely humble us.

Why is humility so crucial when we are bereft? It is because we are tempted to test God, fight against Him, and even turn away from Him in the midst of unanswered prayers and the mantle of mystery under which we dwell. When Sarah was born, I was tempted to ask God to prove His divinity by curing Sarah overnight. The thought occurred to me, "If God is compassionate and truly desires all of us to be healed and whole, then surely He can perform a miracle and heal Sarah so that she can experience a typical life with her peers." I believed this was a legitimate prayer, because I based it on my firmly held conviction that God does perform miracles.

The truth is that God can do anything (which we inherently know), but His will doesn't always coincide with human logic or even our limited capacity for empathy. I wanted to resist what I instinctively recognized as God's will: for Sarah to be born with a rare craniofacial condition that would require complicated and risky surgeries throughout her life, not to mention ridicule and ostracism from her developmental peers and even strangers or passersby. It wasn't that God wanted Sarah to be broken or that He cruelly desired for her to undergo a lifetime of agony (e.g., not His perfect will). Rather, God did will for Sarah her personal path of sanctification, and the cryptic puzzle for me was in accepting that her path would be one of direct and immediate suffering (through His permissive will).

We must ponder the reality of God's will, remembering that He has a perfect and permissive will, both in harmony with each other. Because He is omniscient, He already knew that Sarah would be born with Apert Syndrome. He is also omnipotent, which meant that He could have altered that diagnosis, either prenatally or anytime afterward. He may have perfectly willed for Sarah to have Apert Syndrome, knowing what she would endure, or He may have permissively willed for the genetic muta-tion to occur, also knowing that her journey with a rare condi-tion would be precisely the means by which she would arrive in Heaven someday.

The mystery of this truth was born of a grace-filled moment of humility when the Lord asked me to trust that He was a mu-nificent, all knowing, all powerful Deity whose plan for Sarah involved her ongoing suffering. Humility required me to set aside my agenda, my will, and even my preconceived notions of who God was. I had to admit to myself that I really knew very little about God, that His thoughts were above my thoughts, and His ways surpassed my finite ways (see Isa. 55:9). It was impossible for me to grasp that God could concurrently be all loving, all knowing, and all powerful while Sarah was born with a debilitat-ing condition that had the potential to affect every aspect of her life: cognitive, physiological, spiritual, and emotional.

Humility, therefore, is an aspiration for us to strive for dur-ing the process of grieving. Somehow when we surrender our limited, narrow perception of the infinite God, we are freer to accept His goodness. We are then more capable of noticing the small (yet significant) blessings that He offers us on daily. We are more inclined to deny the world's perspective of suffering and instead embrace the gift of redemptive suffering as we see it lived through our lives and as we are asked to help carry someone else's cross. The degradation in this is that we become Simon the Cyrene, an unassuming bystander thrust into the Passion and forced to carry Jesus' Cross.

Grief holds many dimensions of obscurity and ambiguity. We can choose to accept the unknown factors, the unanswered prayers, the spiritual contradictions and paradoxes, or we can allow our pride to consume us with vexation, ferocity, and vehemence. If we choose the latter, we often close ourselves off to God altogether, because we cannot accept that our human understanding of goodness and mercy may contrast with an unbounded, uncreated Deity. Our pride builds walls around our hearts, while humility crumbles the walls through God's merciful grace.

Love points the way to humility. When we bid God's love to tear down our emotional barricades, healing naturally follows. In turn, our ability to love becomes more altruistic, and we are better able to love others and ourselves with the same gentleness and mercy that God extends to us in our pain (but more on that later).

Father de Bergamo summarized this beautifully as it pertains to isolated (acute) or ongoing (chronic) grief:

> To fix our thoughts solely on our own wretchedness might cause us to fall into self-distrust and despair, and in the same way to fix our thoughts solely on the contemplation of the Divine Goodness might cause us to be

presumptuous and rash. True humility lies between the two: "Humility," says St. Thomas, "checks presumption and strengthens the soul against despair."

Distrust yourself and confide in God, and thus distrusting and thus confiding, between fear and hope, you shall work out your salvation in the spirit of the Gospel.

Bereavement is such a fragile phase of life, so we must tread delicately on our temptation toward despair and fear. If we pray for the grace of humility, God will grant it. We know this in accordance with His perfect will, because humility is the foundational virtue that gives life to all others. It is such a necessary virtue for Heaven, because it requires a constant death to self and openness to God. When we grieve, we may be enraged at our circumstances, which isn't sinful in itself. It becomes sinful only when we turn away from the One who inexorably pursues us. Humility turns us away from losing hope and toward our loving Father. We thrust ourselves into His arms, weeping and thrashing about while He receives us with patience and protection.

Humility lures our hearts toward God when pride would have us believe that we can manage our own destinies without His intervention. Therefore, humility is the virtue we need more than any other when our hearts are in perpetual anguish and we cannot hear another word about good coming from evil. Humility will have us listen and remain open to God even as we are inconsolable by human contact. Cling to humility. Pray for it relentlessly, especially when you are grieving. It will carry you from a place of despondency to hope beyond imagination, and from there you will soar to the heights of new life—a new life lived with meaning in the midst of mystery.

The Grace of Redemptive Suffering

Second Spiritual Principle:
Abandonment to Divine Providence

In his *Abandonment to Divine Providence*, Father Jean-Pierre de Caussade says, "Our only satisfaction must be to live in the present moment as if there were nothing to expect beyond it."[21] The second pillar, or principle, of advancing in our spiritual development through bereavement is that of abandonment to Divine Providence. The focus here is on pleasing God rather than oneself, and this virtue[22] is acquired through acts that try one's patience and foster perseverance.

The concept of abandonment often conjures images of enslavement with a person in shackles and beholden to his master. Divine Providence altogether is another aspect of this spiritual principle, and both together form a celestial image of what it means to be truly free by choosing to relinquish all that we are and all that we have (including our pain) into God's care.

Abandonment is quite the opposite of the suffocating and isolating spiritual servitude that occurs when we sin. Abandonment is a liberating act, because it requires one's free will knowingly to choose self-surrender to God. Because humility is essential to reaching this pillar, it's crucial to note that abandonment cannot occur without at least the seed of humility planted in one's heart. A person who is abandoned to God is entirely empty of self

---

[21] Father Jean-Pierre de Caussade was a beloved French spiritual director during the nineteenth century when the concept of Divine Providence was popular and spreading worldwide. His book *Abandonment to Divine Providence* is the basis of this portion of the chapter.

[22] I use the term *virtue* unofficially, referring not to the theological or cardinal virtues but to these spiritual practices that foster virtue in one's life.

and all vain distractions so that this spiritual nakedness exposes one's soul without shame to the God of the universe — the God who heals.

Divine Providence is altogether another concept that is related to abandonment. Divine, of course, references God, and Providence refers to His intimate care for us. Many people believe in coincidences, while others call these "God-incidents." These seeming flukes are actually deliberate motions of God's hand in our lives. Abandonment to Divine Providence, therefore, is a self-renunciation of our worries and concerns, sins and distractions and a trusting in the infinite care of God, who loves us. This entails us first to believe that God cherishes us so personally that He hears the whispers of our hearts, even the ones that aren't fully formed into a prayer. When we believe this, we learn to rely on God for resolution of all that assails us, from inconsequential grievances to enigmatic tragedies.

This is an act that must be made on a daily basis, sometimes more than once a day, though we will certainly encounter setbacks and obstacles. Patience quiets the tempest within us when we hope to advance more quickly or when we (out of pride) assume we have already advanced to a higher degree of abandonment than reality suggests. God reveals our weaknesses to us so that we can continue to relinquish all to Him and acknowledge our nothingness without Him. Perseverance is also necessary in this pillar because of the temptation to desolation and despair when we perhaps regress on our spiritual walk and when new waves of grief violently and unexpectedly crash against our hearts.

One such wave of grief reminded me of what abandonment looked like in my life. A little girl in the Apert Syndrome community died unexpectedly in her sleep when she was a little over eighteen months old. Like Sarah, she was a fairly exuberant child

with few tangential issues beyond the qualifying characteristics of
everyone born with Apert: craniosynostosis (prematurely fused
cranial plates) and syndactyly (fused fingers and toes). Her death
shocked nearly everyone in the cyber network of Apert families.
Most of us had never met her in person, but nearly all of us had
followed her story.

The grief shredded my heart into a thousand fragments. The
ache was grave and constant for days. Regardless of how I attempted to carry on in an ordinary fashion, it was evident to
me that something had changed. Something had completely
overturned my world, and in order for that throbbing pain to
subside, I knew I had to take a look within.

As I revisited the death of this little girl (named Phoenix), I
realized that I saw so much of Sarah in her. In some ways I had
even projected Sarah's story onto hers. Somewhere in the recesses of my subconscious, I had filed away my own truth: Sarah
was not all that different from Phoenix, and in fact, they were
rather inseparable by medical standards. If one could define a life
solely by one's medical diagnosis, I was confident that Sarah's
and Phoenix's life were nearly identical.

Yet they were entirely separate as unique souls created by a
loving God. I was cognizant of this, yet my heart did not accept
this truth. When I received the notice that Phoenix had passed
on to her eternal reward, I thought of Sarah and the fragility
of her life (more so than the average populace). I considered
all the unknown variables that hovered around our family on
a daily basis: no strong prognosis, no reliable statistics, no cure,
and no known cause.

For one who requires facts, reasons, explanations, and realistic goals, living in the realm of perpetual uncertainty was
agonizing for me. I toyed with various coping mechanisms, the

ones that seemed far less harmful than addiction or suicide, such as busyness, denial, and phony optimism. Somehow I adopted the societal cues that life was just grand, and we were all steadily embracing this new life with ease.

It was difficult to be truthful, even to those closest to us, because people would see Sarah's stellar signature grin and gleefully comment to us, "Sarah looks great. She's doing so well, isn't she?"

Our reply was always a resounding yes, but a skepticism that only Ben and I shared lingered in that response. I knew that, when this child with Apert died, my yes instantly became "I don't know." I understood people's bewilderment, because Sarah appeared healthy and thriving. Necessary surgeries aside, Sarah epitomized the quintessential ideal child: jovial, laid back, and resilient. To those who did not live with a person who had a rare disease, it certainly was perplexing how Sarah seemed to be the picture of health and yet still was vulnerable to developing new medical complications—or even death—at any time.

I couldn't accept this. But when I read about all the parents who had lost children to Apert Syndrome (or related complications), my heart sank into the reality that—any time, any day—this could be Sarah. I always accepted this possibility, especially with the weak statistics that existed about Apert Syndrome and life expectancy, but I had convinced myself that somehow she superseded statistics.

I recall crumpling into a heap of a mess on our family-room floor when Ben was at work and the girls were napping. I couldn't control my sobbing. For the first time I was suffocating in a fear I had once suppressed for the sake of maintaining my sanity in the midst of crisis management, but God permitted me this rare and fleeting opportunity to accept the fragility of Sarah's life and to choose to live in the present moment.

The Grace of Redemptive Suffering

The oppression of fretting about all the unknown factors I was demanding to comprehend about Apert Syndrome—the evidence of surgical success rates, the average mortality and life-expectancy rates, and a mélange of other related data—was unattainable. No one could answer my questions, and in the midst of plausible worry, I had to make a decision to abdicate my will, my thoughts, and even my natural disposition into God's hands. I realized as I reached this apex that all of life—Sarah's life, my life, and every human life—was delicate. Some things were simply a mystery, and I had to accept that life lived within a mystery could still be a life fulfilled.

That day I began consciously opting to live in the here and now rather than wrap my mind around an ambiguous future for Sarah or commiserate over the regrets of my past. It was a foreign concept to me, and yet it liberated me in so many ways. I was finally free to notice the quiet and simple ways that God spoke to me: in the first spring flower, the rustling of the leaves through the trees, or sunshine in a clear, cerulean sky with translucent clouds and a revitalizing breeze, or a little robin nestled outside my window.

It was the robin that brought alive the verse from Matthew 6:26, which is a perfect scriptural illustration of God's providence. The Scripture came to my mind one day as I observed the little female robin cozily burrowed in the nest she had built earlier that day. I pondered the meaning of this verse: "Look at the birds of the air: they neither sow nor reap nor gather into barns, and yet your heavenly Father feeds them. Are you not of more value than they?" This passage reminds us that God cares for the details of your life and mine, the very same minutiae we attempt to manipulate, control, and eliminate. God is aware of everything about us (even the parts of ourselves that remain indecipherable to us), and even more, He cares so personally for you and me that He intervenes in ways we don't realize or comprehend. If God provides food and shelter to the unassuming birds, such as the robin outside my kitchen window, we have to remember that we are worth more than many little birds. God's care for us far outweighs the meager pieces of straw and earthworms that sheltered and sustained the robin. It is a lesson in what Divine Providence means, and what abandoning ourselves to God's will every day might look like.

In abandoning Sarah's future to God's care without the definite knowledge that she would live a long, full life, I allowed God to release decades of despotic spiritual chains that burdened my heart without respite. I was able to enjoy each new day that God gave us with Sarah, despite the unwelcome truth that He could choose to take her home to Him any time. Without "living in the present moment as if there were nothing to expect beyond it," as Father de Caussade succinctly offers, I completely disregarded the blessings of her life today.

Naturally, this applies to every dimension of our lives. We all want answers in the midst of crises. We force solutions and are data-driven in our frenetic society. The intemperance between instant gratification and sloth that we face daily has somehow swept away our chance at enjoying what we are given in this flicker of time.

When we abandon ourselves entirely to God, we achieve a state of serenity and an interior sanctity that all of the saints acquired while they remained on earth. Abandonment to Divine Providence initially requires a constant, conscious act of surrendering our will to God's will, even when His will remains unknown and mysterious. Over time, however, abandonment (when practiced daily) becomes more natural and even perhaps automatic in response to life's messes and chaos. It is this type of abandonment in which our souls rest in harmony with God, our hearts united to His.

Father Jean C. J. d'Elbée beckons us to consider how abandonment to Providence builds on the virtue of humility:

> Abandonment ... requires a great humility, since it is submission of ourselves to creatures and events, seeing Jesus Himself in them.... Abandonment is nothing but obedience pushed to its extreme, since it consists of submission to everything within the limits of the possible and the reasonable, in order to obey God, who has foreseen and willed it all.[23]

Could this truly be the case? We may fight the necessity of abandonment out of fear or pride, constantly pushing ourselves to let go and hand all our thoughts, behaviors, and will to God's care, and yet we may always do so with great resentment and anxiety. This clearly is not true abandonment. At some point in our path to sanctification, we must recognize that true abandonment is the natural result of love for God. Its motivation is love, not force or fear. When we fight ourselves and force ourselves to submit to uncertainties and even abhorrent atrocities in life, we are not practicing authentic abandonment.

We may find ourselves offering God great trust and faith in Him during trying and cumbersome phases of life, when in the past it took great effort to offer much of anything to God except a desire to surrender all to Him. Of course, this desire is

[23] Father Jean C. J. d'Elbée, *I Believe in Love: A Personal Retreat Based on the Teaching of St. Thérèse of Lisieux* (Manchester, NH: Sophia Institute Press, 2001), 84.

the beginning of true abandonment, and it does, in fact, please God when we make this effort. But it is not a complete act of the heart, only a beginning effort of the will.

As an act of the heart, abandonment to Divine Providence requires immense and intense confidence in God, because we have no way of knowing when or how He will choose to act. In pivotal times of confusion or moments when life is dark and bleak, when all seems lost and we feel prone to despair, our hearts must unite completely with God's, to be consumed by the flames of His love so that they will purify and purge our fears, wounds, and sins. When this occurs, our hearts are liberated, and so are our minds and souls. We are free to trust that God truly cares for every component of our lives, and either His perfect or permissive will is at work every moment for the purpose of our personal sanctification.

Grief, then, is the impetus that inserts us into a realm of living these spiritual tenets instead of simply learning about them. After we begin to practice humility and when we understand the desert moments of our faith, God adds this element of abandoning all of our lives—every fragment and aspect—into His care. His provision never fails us, although there are times we may wonder if we have been forsaken by Him. Grief manifests a heinous and brutal dimension of our human nature, but God, in His Mercy, draws us to His heart and presses us there when we want to act on our vexation and rage. God may discipline and prune us through our grief, but the principle of abandonment to Divine Providence teaches us that grief does not have the final say in our lives.

Abandonment occurs shortly before we enter the active and passive night of the soul (more on this soon). Somehow it's not as difficult to lose all (self) for the sake of gaining all (God) once God has begun stripping us of vices, falsehoods, and sensory delights. Abandonment requires incredible trust in God, particularly when no answers are available to our travails. This principle necessarily assumes that everything can be used for the good of our souls, including unfathomable and seemingly cruel life events.

Grief starkly displays those life events so that we are tempted to believe that God is detached from our reality or, even worse, is punishing us severely. Abandonment assumes that God never wishes ill or harm upon anyone and that He uses our suffering to draw us nearer to Him. We cannot empathize with other people's pain if we have not experienced loss firsthand. Abandonment teaches us that grief can become our friend as we persevere in faith.

The heresy of deism claims that God is like a craftsman who created His masterpiece and then abandoned the daily maintenance and operation of His creation. Deists declare, too, that God is some incomprehensible supernatural being who lives high in His Heaven but has no personal involvement in the lives of His people. Christians, on the other hand, believe in a personal God who intimately and lovingly participates in everyone's lives on a moment-to-moment basis. The temptation to believe that God is distant and ephemeral may occur shortly after we experience loss, but the value in clinging to the truth of an active, personal God makes it less nebulous for us to sacrifice everything to Him.

God may seem distant or nonexistent when particular types of tragedies strike. How can any of us—who are fallible—justify a child's suffering from a malignant tumor, let alone an infallible and perfectly loving God (who is Love Himself)? What about the devout couple who longs for a baby and yet has lost seven children through miscarriages? These, and many more examples, bewilder us, because they don't fit the context of a personal God who loves us all impartially.

However trite it may seem, we must persevere in both faith and trust in God, knowing that He does, in fact, love the child with cancer and the childless couple as much as He loves the healthy child and the couple with several children. Believing that God *is*, and we *are not*, is a form of abandonment, because we acknowledge that life and love are inadequately known to us. God alone knows His reasons, and we trust Him along the way rather than give in to despair.

Third Spiritual Principle: Holy Indifference

"If it happens that the soul is attached or inclined to a thing inordinately," says St. Ignatius of Loyola, "that [person] should move himself, putting forth all his strength, to come to the contrary of what he is wrongly drawn to."[24]

The third spiritual pillar that leads us away from bitterness in our grief and toward a higher purpose is the concept of holy indifference. Here we focus on choosing God's will rather than our will in circumstances that present a favorable option and an unfavorable option that directly contradicts our will.

The concept of *holy indifference* may befuddle us when we first stumble upon it, because we can't fathom being indifferent about anything (especially if we are of choleric temperament). It may not be ingrained in our genetic wiring to be lax or moderate,

---

[24] St. Ignatius of Loyola, *The Spiritual Exercises*, annotation 16. Considered a spiritual classic, *The Spiritual Exercises* was St. Ignatius of Loyola's magnum opus and for hundreds of years has been a well-beloved treatise on advancing in one's interior life.

although we may be advised to learn moderation from influential people in our lives. Indifference may at first seem to indicate the lukewarm person about whom Jesus spoke: the one who, since he is neither hot nor cold, should be spit out of Jesus' mouth (see Rev. 3:16).

Such strong language may not deter us from setting lofty goals and convincing ourselves that it is plausible for us to attain them without much effort. St. Ignatius's conversion was quite radical: he went from one extreme to another—from a life of luxury, excess, and pleasure to an austere life of poverty. His heart was set ablaze (much like mine was), and I pondered the ways in which he overcame his nature of extremes. I knew God was calling me on a similar path, one of spiritual moderation and emotional harmony, but I didn't know where to begin or how to obtain it with the level of perseverance I knew would be required of me.

Ignatian spirituality asks: What is man's final end? This is the foundation of the concept of holy indifference, that condition of neither desiring nor possessing anyone or anything except God. St. Ignatius's way is truly one of ascetical theology. In my life, holy indifference certainly wasn't lived from day to day. It was an irrelevant and distasteful concept, because my understanding of the beauty of holy indifference was skewed and incomplete.

A related spiritual guidepost to holy indifference is holy detachment, which is also connected to the annihilation of self-will. Naturally, this third principle develops as one advances in both humility and daily abandonment to God's providence. This struggle—holy indifference—usually arrives when we have been coasting for a time without many impediments to our interior progress. Unholy attachments often surface in the form of one's will and intellect (e.g., pride again), which initially causes sadness but which eventually becomes interior tranquillity through the refinement of holy indifference.

Consider this poignant reflection from Dom Vitalis Lehodey, O.C.R.:[25]

> There is the radical evil of undue attachment to one's own judgment and one's own will. This is the poisoned source of all our sins and imperfections. How few know how to trace their particular maladies to this fountain-head of every disorder! Only too often is it not self-judgment that pretends to prescribe the remedy, and self-will that sees to the application, while, on the contrary, it is just self-judgment and self-will that should be sacrificed without mercy and first of all? Providence will help us to correct such errors or such weakness....
>
> [God] desires to keep us constantly disposed to renounce our judgments and to immolate our wills. Therefore he is careful to conceal his designs from us. Very often he will proceed in a manner contrary to our anticipations and ideas, and will directly attack both our tastes and repugnances. If we wish to examine the matter closely we shall find that he does nothing without a very definite purpose.

Consider Lehodey's strong rhetoric about self-will as it relates to self-assessment: a "radical evil." So vehemently are we affixed to ourselves (our worldview, our personality and its expression, and even our fears and failures) that it is rather impossible for

---

[25] Reverend Abbot Dom Vitalis Lehodey, O.C.R., *The Dom Vitalis Lehodey Collection*, 2 vols. (London: Catholic Way Publishing, 2015), chap. 1.

holy indifference to penetrate us through God's grace if we do not renounce all that is distasteful to our senses and contrary to our inclinations. This is why God often operates through circumstances that directly violate our self-will; what appears to be a flagrant slap in the face is, in actuality, a holy opportunity to advance in this spiritual principle. Holy indifference happens when we intentionally sacrifice what we want in favor of perhaps an unknown outcome to a decision or situation, knowing that this purgation draws us nearer to love of God and an authentic desire for His holy will in all things.

Likewise, our unholy bond to self-will initially strikes us with a wave of sadness when God removes our attachments. This is particularly evident in grief: we lose someone (or something) to whom (or to which) we have become connected, and we don't want the loss of that person or thing. Sadness ensues. We may tousle with this emotion for a time, but if we remain in this state of sorrow, we are slaves to self-will and do not experience authentic freedom, the freedom God longs for us to possess.

Father Tadeusz Dajczer explains this portion of our third principle quite eloquently:

> An obvious *sign of attachments* is also your *sadness in situations when God takes something away from you.* He, will, therefore, take that by which you are enslaved—hence everything that is your greatest enemy, that which causes your heart not to be free for him. It is when you start to accept this and do it cheerfully that you will become more and more free.
>
> During prayer in the presence of the Lord, show him not only your empty but also dirty hands, defiled by the attachments to mammon, and pray that he will have

mercy on you. Prayer can develop only in the atmosphere of freedom.[26]

If we truly desire healing in the midst of our losses, we must cultivate the space for prayer to occur, which is cleared when we present our filthiness and vacuity to God—realizing our gratuitous attachment to our own will. In that space, our capacity for genuine prayer develops, and we finally experience the release of our burdens through the freedom God waits for us to claim.

God opened the door of my heart to Ignatian spirituality from the military perspective. Because I had always longed to be a soldier for Christ (which was more likely a romantic notion than a noble, holy one), I learned more about the spiritual allegory of the soldier. I conjured the image of an ongoing battle, for I was always a believer in spiritual warfare. I sensed the angels and saints engaging in an intense crusade around me, somewhere in the realm I knew existed and yet could not visualize with my senses.

At one point, I made a decision to choose the same level of heroism that a soldier fighting for his life—and the lives of those around him—would choose. I wanted to exhibit that degree of virtue in my life, yet I knew I was missing a critical component. Where was the missing link, the lost key? In my spiritual immaturity, I didn't realize the necessity of purgation. Impulsivity (sadly) is diametrically opposed to humble and joyful waiting as our souls are refined in the fire. This obvious spiritual truth had not yet taken hold of my soul, however. This was my missing link, staring me in the face, but I was too young, fickle, and proud to recognize it.

---

[26] Excerpted from the *Meditation of the Day* in the <u>Magnificat</u> from November 7, 2015 (with original emphasis).

The Grace of Redemptive Suffering

Not until I became well acquainted with St. Ignatius did I begin to grasp how holy indifference manifested itself in my life. It unfolded gradually, but it was during periods of silent and vigilant waiting that I became aware of my unholy attachments. I was very territorial of my earthly possessions and was always careful to safeguard my professional and personal reputation. I couldn't surrender my dreams and plans for my future. Everything in my life was held by my unwavering grip, and I did not let go earnestly—or even willingly at first.

I discovered that my attachments, although certainly sinful, were motivated by fear. I was afraid to lose myself somehow if I lost what I had acquired in my life. At the time, my identity was rooted in my accomplishments, accolades, possessions, and so forth. Fear drove me to a state of spiritual catatonia and eventual paralysis. If I could not instantaneously become a valiant soldier for Christ, I could not move at all. That was how I lived: all or nothing. The middle ground, moderation, holy indifference—it was all like learning a foreign language.

Over the course of many years, I realized the gift of intentionality of passion. Passion undirected becomes misguided and turns to folly, but passion that is tested and purged of its carnal tendencies converts to wisdom. In this way, we who are aggrieved learn that temperance enables us to let go of the outcome of seemingly troublesome and unwelcome situations. Holy indifference moderates that passion, squelching it just enough to liberate our hearts from expecting life to go as we, rather than God, had planned.

In retrospect, it is abundantly clear that God was building the necessary spiritual foundation for me to be prepared for the challenges that lay ahead with our daughters. First I had to incorporate the understanding of authentic love that is refined during the holy darkness, and then it was critical that I lived in a state of holy indifference. Because Sarah's condition is so rare, I learned very quickly that I needed to surrender the outcome of every detail of my life into God's hands, without specific expectations.

This is also important when we are in bereavement. So often we tend to cling to whatever amount of control we can muster over our lives: maintaining a flawless house, creating exquisite culinary concoctions, organizing and cleaning the garage, and so forth. The external loci of control we exhibit is simply a mask for our desperation at what we are unable to manage on our own, which are often the bigger pieces of our lives.

Holy indifference, then, is a way in which we can learn how to surrender each moment of uncertainty and anxiety into God's loving care. We may petition God, secretly hoping for a specific answer or outcome to our prayer, but with a soul filled with holy indifference, nothing is difficult or causes unnecessary fretting and weeping. An indifferent soul knows that God wills *our good*, so it is content with favorable or unfavorable circumstances. This knowledge is what assists the soul through tragedy, because it is an ever-present reminder that beauty and meaning can be found in the midst of intense loss and pain.

We recall, perhaps nostalgically, the ways in which we have loved and lost. When we watch the transformation of a loved one who is preparing for eternity, the beauty of a soul in a state of grace is never more evident. It is as if that person's soul becomes visible in his or her face, and we notice a striking and transcendent peace that transfigures him or her as death draws near. Sometimes, too, unresolved conflicts that may have perpetuated over the course of many decades suddenly surface when relatives gather to say goodbye to this dying loved one, and when resolution occurs in the spirit of forgiveness and love, beauty exists in that loss.

This doesn't mean that we are apathetic toward suffering or toward those who approach us with specific prayer requests. It simply means we have no interior attachment to our will. In fact, our will becomes extinguished throughout the dark night of our senses and soul so that we abdicate our longings and hopes in favor of God's plan for our lives. There is incredible freedom in this way of being. In fact, we may not be privy to God's will for our prayers, yet we remain undaunted and, in fact, serene. A quiet confidence rests within us when we resign ourselves and our future to the God of the universe.

Our hearts can rest in the "peace that surpasses all understanding" (cf. Phil. 4:7) because we know that God will use the results for our good. Applying this spiritual principle has been the single most influential part of my life as a caregiver when dealing with the messiness of grief, because grief is so unpredictable and often unheralded. Grief is the instructor that facilitates growth in holy indifference, because it forces us to release what worries and ails us.

Loss of any kind can thrust us into a state of spiritual or emotional barrenness, which may initially frustrate us. Our hearts pang for life to resume as it once was, and we long for the void to be filled with comforts and consolations. When none is given, we may attempt, out of desperation, to cleave to what we know and understand. We seek safety and security, but instead we find ourselves lost and terrified. Holy indifference is the opportunity here. It is the light, the salve, the refreshment we need to bring some sense to what is senseless.

God is asking us to trust, which involves a stepping back from the details we try to micromanage. Holy indifference is a concept that invites us to enter the mystery of life and to dwell there, safely and securely, in the womb of the unknown. God holds us there, nestled in the chrysalis of waiting, and we grow closer to Him without realizing it. This happens when we pray with confidence, knowing that whatever may come is for our good.

Fourth Spiritual Principle: The Dark Night

To come to the pleasure you have not,
    You must go by a way in which you enjoy not.
To come to the knowledge you have not,
    You must go by a way in which you know not.
To come to the possession you have not,
    You must go by a way in which you possess not.
To come to be what you are not,
    You must go by a way in which you are not. [27]

This fourth pillar of spiritual advancement in grief is focused on fidelity to God in the face of self-emptiness. It is acquired through time, temptations, trials, and tribulations. Let us examine this principle, which builds on the previous three, according St. John of the Cross's mystical theology, whose pertinence for those in mourning is indisputable.

Some saints have found a sure, quick, and easy way to Heaven. But St. John of the Cross never alleged that his way was an easy road to eternal life. In fact, he asserted quite the opposite. He frankly posited that most people who wrestled with the dark night of the soul would, in fact, be treading in a direction that

---

[27] St. John of the Cross, sketch of Mount Carmel. St. John of the Cross sketched in Spanish a diagram of how he visualized the ascent of a soul from Earth to Heaven. It is a rough image that was eventually translated into English and incorporated into his classic *Collected Works*, intended to be a preface for *The Ascent to Mount Carmel*.

would cause strain and death to the senses, the will, and the intellect.

Another renowned spiritual writer, Thomas à Kempis, further explained why our anxieties and fluctuations between "hope and fear" thwart our spiritual progress. The main cause of this impediment to full union with God is our tepidity toward the discipline necessary to achieve it.

> There is one thing that keeps many back from spiritual progress, and from fervor in amendment: namely, the labor that is necessary for the struggle. And assuredly they especially advance beyond others in virtues, who strive the most manfully to overcome the very things which are the hardest and most contrary to them. For there a man does profit more and merit more abundant grace, when he does most to overcome himself and mortify his spirit.[28]

When a person enters the dark night, it is an arduous path to Heaven, at least for a time. Grief very much feels this way: that our thoughts, our emotions, our very livelihood are encapsulated in darkness. This makes traversing through that darkness cumbersome and painful, but fidelity to God in the midst of such spiritual fog enables us to persevere through the trials of suffering. We merely need to begin with a desire for the "labor necessary for the struggle."

My former spiritual director recommended that I read St. John of the Cross's collected works after many weeks of uncertainty in discerning a new course for my life. I sensed I was on the cusp of an epiphany, but I was unsure what it was or how I would recognize it once it arrived. In the past, my ability to

---

[28] Thomas à Kempis, *The Imitation of Christ*, bk. 1, chap. 25.

discern God's will had been fairly direct, but at the point of receiving spiritual direction, practically everything in my life had become murky and nebulous. Everyday choices were tedious, and major decisions were too cumbersome even to dare to approach.

St. John of the Cross profoundly and permanently changed my life. What I learned from the very beginning is that some (but not all) souls are called into what he termed as the "dark night" of the senses and spirit. God determines that certain people obtain their unique call to sanctification by sojourning through the darkening of the senses, will, memory, and intellect. Other souls may benefit from a contrasting spiritual journey. Regardless of how a soul achieves its eternal reward, *this* way—the purgative darkening of the soul—is a path that a soul does not select for itself, but is rather beckoned to enter by God.

There are two basic types of darkness: darkness caused by the consequences of sin and eternal death, and a holy darkness. The holy darkness is the one about which St. John of the Cross writes extensively, but both deserve a bit more elaboration.

When we are in the throes of ongoing mourning, it is difficult to differentiate between the darkness of sin and evil and holy darkness. At times, both may appear to be one and the same, and all we know is that we are entangled in a place where nothingness exists. We see nothing, hear nothing, know little, and seem to make no progress in our spiritual lives. We are sensitive to pain, and our hearts are continually shredded by the suffering we endure (or have seen others endure) with no apparent reprieve.

It is understandable why we may initially believe that darkness is darkness, and there are no distinguishable differences in it. If it is the absence of light, hope, and wholeness, what does it matter if darkness is caused by sin and evil or is actually the light of God shining in our souls? Their divergent characteristics are critical, precisely because of our *response* to them. When we know what type of darkness is occurring, we know more clearly how we can approach it.

The psalmist declares:

If I say, "Let only darkness cover me,
    and the light about me be night,"
even the darkness is not dark to thee,
    the night is bright as the day;
    for darkness is as light with thee. (Ps. 139:11–12)

To God, there is no darkness. Even the darkness He allows to envelop us elucidates our grieving and wounded hearts. St. John of the Cross knew this well, and he used examples from Scripture (similar to this one) to elaborate the allegory of holy darkness.

When my daughter Sarah was born with Apert Syndrome, I considered all the healthy babies who were born with ten fingers and ten toes. I looked at Sarah and immediately intuited that her life would be riddled with surgeries, pain management, and postoperative healing. As a mother I had to acknowledge that her syndrome was contrary to the natural order of birth and growth in humanity. She was considered to be a medical anomaly, and the underlying message was always that "she wasn't supposed to be this way." My thoughts naturally centered on the question *why*: *Why* was Sarah born with fused fingers instead of separated ones? *Why* wasn't she born healthy and whole as most children are?

I received no easy answers to my questions. I knew I could not direct them at secular individuals who would proffer shallow and hollow replies. There were moments in the stillness of cognition when I mulled over the first sin and the consequences to all of creation because of the infection of sin.

It's true that all of creation reflects the decision of our first parents. We see it in diseases of crops, bizarre weather patterns, pestilence and plagues, and the eventual death of all living things. Without sounding apocalyptic, the imperfection of all creation resounds in the fore of our psyches at all times. On a daily basis we encounter the flaws and foibles in people and in nature. Because we know that God made all things good and perfectly pleasing to Him, we also know that the consequences of original sin have stained all of creation, as well.

We can also attest to the reality of darkness in the form of evil. All of us have seen, heard of, or experienced the horrors of violence in unimaginable forms. We turn on the evening news and are constantly bombarded with images of assault, increasingly disturbing and bizarre acts of terror, murder, neglect, and abuse. Our pop culture reflects this type of darkness in its music, television shows, and books.

In this regard, God gave mankind the ultimate gift of love when He permitted us to choose what is good, holy, and true or to choose destruction and death. We choose to respond to circumstances out of our control. One of my favorite verses that substantiates this belief is from Deuteronomy 30:19: "I have set before you life and death, blessing and curse; therefore choose life, that you and your descendants may live."

This is the first type of darkness—the tainted effects on the environment and on our human nature—is a consequence of sin. This is not a holy darkness. It is the kind of darkness we tend to assign to anything that is unfavorable to our natural tendencies. Whatever exists outside of the realm of comfort, pleasure, or the accumulation of wealth and health, we consider to be categorized as an unholy darkness.

Not all suffering is unholy, however. This is why St. John of the Cross eloquently draws to our attention the existence of a very beautiful and necessary darkness. It is set apart from the darkness of sin and death, because it is a specific spiritual journey that God permits some of us to undergo as a means for our ultimate sanctification. All of us (at the very least) briefly collide with the concept of the dark night of the soul when we experience both acute and chronic grief. Still others dwell in this dark night completely outside of the bounds of grief, in a realm of suffering for the sake of love.

Theologically, St. John of the Cross explains that the dark night of the soul is both passive and active and begins during the purgative stage of mystical union.[29] The *Dark Night of the Soul* is most likely St. John of the Cross's most well-known and oft-quoted treatise on the concept of holy darkness. But St. John's first magnum opus, the *Ascent of Mount Carmel*, actually laid the foundation for the spiritual seeker to grasp more clearly the ultimate reality of the dark night of the soul. According to scholars of St. John's work, the *Ascent* displays the active night of the spirit, while the dark night illustrates the passive aspect of darkness.[30]

[29] Most mystical writers define three states of spiritual advancement: the purgative, illuminative, and unitive ways. St. John of the Cross was among those who specified what these stages might look like for a soul.

[30] St John of the Cross, *Collected Works of St. John of the Cross*, trans. Kieran Kavanaugh, OCD and Otilio Rodriguez, OCD (Wilmington, DE: ICS Publications, 1991), 57. An interesting and critical note is that the dark night is considered the first step

How can one recognize a holy darkness, as opposed to the darkness of illness or sin? Holy darkness is an offering from God to develop total union, or infusion, of our soul with Him. The dark night of the soul is not contingent on wavering emotions, heightened senses, or external rewards. When a person is in the state of spiritual infancy, God often delights the soul with the sweetness of consolations, visions, mystical experiences, signs, and other confirmations of His presence. However, there comes a point when the spiritual person hits a patch of aridity, perhaps in completing prayers or the desire to attend Mass and receive the sacraments. There is no longer any gratification derived in these behaviors and rituals, so that person is tempted to discontinue the spiritual practices that once were sweet and have somehow become dry.

If a person perseveres through the initial strains of the spiritual desert, the soul receives boundless graces and grows magnanimously in virtue. However, the person who is in the midst of a holy darkness will be entirely unaware of these gifts and blessings, because he or she can only (rightly) recognize his or her sinfulness, struggles, and weaknesses. Others may note how a person appears to be growing in holiness, but to the one whose soul has been withdrawn from practical knowledge and awareness, all is murky and nebulous, except one's sins and grief.

of the purgative way to spiritual union with God. The second level is the illuminative way, and the final stage is the unitive way. The *Ascent of Mount Carmel* and the *Dark Night of the Soul* primarily focus on the purgative way while weaving concepts about the illuminative and unitive ways throughout both texts. The three paths to spiritual intimacy with God deserve a comprehensive overview that is separate from this book.

St. John of the Cross explains that the active night of the soul involves a person's consent, and one pursues means of mortification through the theological virtues. In the beginning, one's senses must be purged. Then the journey of faith follows, and subsequently the memory (where hope is born), and the will (where charity is nurtured) are stripped of all thoughts, longing, and desires that do not lead to God.

The passive night is where the dark night ensues. This is a much darker chasm than the primary mortification of the senses, memory, intellect, and will. In essence, a person's soul has been obscured by a painful longing for God that remains unfulfilled by any activity or human relationship one previously enjoyed. The pining is the suffering of the soul, for the person neither sees nor experiences God in an overt manner. No longer does the soul recognize the sweetness of consolation or the direct light of clarity through signs or mystical revelations. One feels lost, lonely, and uncertain. God seems distant and quiet.

Although a person may believe he or she is forsaken by God at this point, the contrary is true. Herein lies the enigma: we are more closely united to God the more separated we believe we are to be from Him. This is true *only* for a soul that has entered the dark night of the spirit, *not* for a soul that has separated itself from God's grace due to unconfessed mortal sin. This is why the distinction between a holy and unholy darkness is imperative.

St. John explains the interior tumult of a soul in the midst of the dark night in this way:

> The soul, if it desires to pay close attention, will clearly recognize how on this road it suffers many ups and downs, and how immediately after prosperity some tempest and trial follows, so much so that seemingly that calm was

given to forewarn and strengthen it against the future penury; it sees too how abundance and tranquility succeed misery and torment, and in suchwise that it thinks it was made to fast before celebrating that feast.

This is the ordinary procedure in the state of contemplation until one arrives at quietude; the soul never remains in one state, but everything is ascent and descent.[31]

We can see how the inner turmoil, the highs and lows we feel when we are grieving, are possibly reflections of this state of spiritual advancement. How can we know definitively that we haven't fallen on the path of perdition when all is black, and we are certain of very little, if anything? We may wonder if this is even probable, considering the battle we are fighting within ourselves.

A person can be certain that his or her soul is *not* suffering an unholy darkness when he or she remains faithful to the tenets of the Church and is in a state of grace. The sacraments are often the only consolation one receives when the soul grieves for a time. There is no way to tell when the soul will be released from the holy darkness, but obedience and perseverance in faith is the key to withstanding the storms of grief that afflict and crucify the soul.

Not everyone encounters this dark night, but grief is akin to this spiritual concept, because a bereaved person knows well the gravity of the heart's affliction when all seems lost and gone forever. The heart is inconsolable when it is grief stricken. Because the state of grief is similar to the holy darkness that St. John of the Cross defined, it is critical that one who is bereft

[31] *Collected Works of St. John of the Cross*, 372.

hurls himself or herself into the arms of God—with reflection and desperation.

When we turn away from God in periods of mourning, we miss the opportunity to grow closer to Him. We completely reject His offering of love. I was never in a darker place than after Sarah was born, but also have I never learned a greater love than in walking this path of self-denial and chronic grief. In suffering, the gem of pure love is discovered, but few of us recognize this treasure. It is illogical, so our natural impulse is to run from the darkness rather than to enter into it and abandon ourselves with confidence and trust in God.

When I was asking myself the hard questions about why Sarah was chosen to be born with her genetic condition, I returned to the very rudimentary theological tenets of my early religious education. I had to ask myself if I *truly* believed that God was omniscient, omnipotent, and omnipresent. I knew He was always present, and I also knew He was all powerful and all knowing.

But is God *all loving* too? It may take time for us to accept that His mercy appears to us in the disguise of suffering—in essence, our cross—and when we come to the crux of embracing rather than rejecting the gift of our cross, we come to be infused with His endless mercies and love.

When we grieve, we do not feel God's closeness all the time. We may not even believe He truly loves us if He permits us to endure such excruciating agony, especially if our grief is chronic. Sometimes our grief may last a lifetime, in fact. We can choose to become hardened by the world's explanation of suffering, or we can opt to contradict our human reasoning and accept the mystery of the cross.

Love is always hidden in suffering. Love is fulfilled in suffering. The words of St. John of the Cross ring true in our lives, however odd they sound to human nature: "To come to be what you are not, you must go by a way in which you know not."

When we are grief stricken, we must remember that we have entered a particular way of being and living that seems counter-intuitive and unnatural, perhaps even unfamiliar. This is the way in which we "know not." It's that act of trust in moving forward instead of regressing or even becoming stagnant in our spiritual development that leads us to become more than what we are today, "to come to be what you are not."

Fifth Spiritual Principle: Confidence in God's Timing
"One weakness we all have to guard against is worry," says Venerable Solanus Casey. "Instead of worrying we would do well to foster confidence in God. This we can do by not only patience, but by thanking God ahead of time for whatever He sees is best for us.... Courage is half the battle—confidence in God is the soul of prayer—foster the latter and you have both."[32]

The fifth principle is quite possibly the climax of our spiritual advancement toward interior freedom and wholeness subsequent to loss and paves the way for the illuminative state of spiritual union with God. Here the focus is on gratitude instead of envy or anger (both of which may be internalized as guilt). It is acquired through conscious efforts to praise and thank God in the midst of difficulty and uncertainty. Gratitude changes everything, especially when we are grieving: our focus, our perspective, our attitude. Father Solanus Casey knew this well and was able to articulate it not only through his sagacious eloquence but more so in the ways he truly lived this principle.

[32] Catherine M. Odell, *Father Solanus: The Story of Solanus Casey, O.F.M. Cap.* (Huntington, IN: Our Sunday Visitor, 1995), 32.

I used to believe that thanking God before a prayer was answered was presumptuous. Most of my prayers during my spiritual infancy were fairly one-dimensional and self-absorbed. Like most children, I often requested that certain things would turn out the way I wanted or that I would obtain a certain grade on an exam or receive a long-awaited toy for Christmas. Even into young adulthood, my petitions to God were self-important reverberations of what I wanted, when, and how.

I am a self-described control freak. Perhaps a more muted description would be that I am a perfectionist and a worrier. I was born fretting about everything within myself and in my immediate surroundings. I wanted everything to fit neatly into a box, so that few, if any, surprises would startle me or interfere with my predictable, safe existence.

Life was less strenuous while I categorized myself and attempted to predict and plan for disasters or potential catastrophes. Of course, the older I grew, the more I realized that life itself was unpredictable, complex, and messy.

And God works in the unexplained. God is a God of surprises and adventures. He often operates at seemingly inconvenient times and in what we may deem as impulsive ways. However, what appear to be His spontaneous movements are actually deliberate.

He is a God of intentionality. He is a God of providence. The ways in which God provides for us may seem disordered and inconvenient, because the workings of the Holy Spirit are based on timing and need. As a child, I was mindful of this but did not live it in my interior life—that is, not until my parents illustrated for my brother and me a lesson in trusting in God's perfect timing and having confidence that He would provide for us in dire situations.

Despite my parents' unwavering confidence in God, I continued to battle anxieties. Each time I saw or heard of something horrific happening to a person or a community, I would panic inside. The *what ifs* stormed through my head with impending doom. I fabricated in my mind every fathomable disaster with fury and fear. As with nearly everything else in my life, I suppressed these fears, because I recognized their irrational nature. Ironically, I didn't want to be labeled, even though I labeled everything in my life so as to make it comfortable and familiar to me.

But labels slowly eroded over time. It was when I was on this threshold of a spiritual renewal and deepening of faith that I was introduced to the life of Father Solanus Casey.

He was born of Irish immigrant parents who raised several children. Solanus grew up poor, and at one point his family lived in a crude one-room abode with a dirt floor when they left the east coast to establish a farm in the north-central United States.

Solanus was a simpleminded child and retained his guileless nature throughout young adulthood, when he discovered his call to the priesthood. After much deliberation, he discerned that he was called to the community of the Capuchin Franciscans. Yet the friary proved to be a challenging environment for Father Solanus. He was often chided and scorned for his simplicity, which other priests interpreted as ignorance of the Faith.

Despite the constant stream of taunts and admonitions, Father Solanus performed his assigned duties wholeheartedly and cheerfully. Most of these would have been degrading and humiliating to an ordained priest, but not to Father Solanus. He scrubbed toilets and acted as doorkeeper without dismay and certainly not grudgingly. As a result, he was able to interface with the community of laity who frequented the friary for day pilgrimages, retreats, Mass, and spiritual direction. His amiable disposition attracted many spiritual seekers, and eventually Father Solanus had a full-fledged ministry simply by acting as doorkeeper of the friary.

Father Solanus was infused with the charisms of knowledge and counsel, and he demonstrated the ability to assist people in holy discernment through the fracases and disturbances of life. He often simply listened to people, interacted with them, and smiled at them after greeting them at the entrance of the friary. Over time, however, hundreds of people would explicitly seek out Father Solanus, because his unpretentious and unintended spiritual direction proved to be fruitful in their lives. In turn, he wrote many letters offering prayer support and simple spiritual advice to those he could not visit in person.

Naturally, as is the case with many holy people, Father Solanus carried a heavy cross of which few were aware. He developed physical maladies that caused severe pain when he walked or stood for long period. But because he bore his sufferings without a hint of difficulty, those dwelling in his community with a business-as-usual attitude were surprised to learn about his afflictions after his death.

Father Solanus Casey's last words were, "I give my soul to Jesus Christ."[33]

When I read about Father Solanus Casey's life, I was deeply moved and felt an instant spiritual kinship with him. I was convinced that his sanctity displayed on earth was duly rewarded in Heaven. His simplicity beguiled me into strengthening my

---

[33] O'Dell, *Father Solanus*, 229.

somewhat complacent faith at the time, but what intrigued me most of all were his words "Thank God ahead of time."

By thanking God ahead of time, we acknowledge that God is a God of goodness. We reiterate the truth that He is omnipotent, omniscient, and omnipresent. Thanksgiving is often offered *following* a blessing in one's life. But Father Solanus wasn't just speaking of blessings as cause for gratitude. He was implying that we must thank God for everything—the good and the (perceived) bad—*before* it occurs.

When we thank God ahead of time, we lift up a simple, yet profound, oblation that contains a deep-seated comprehension of God's love for us. We are saying that, beyond a shadow of a doubt, we know that "all things work for *good* for those who love God, who are called according to his purpose" (Rom. 8:28, NAB, emphasis mine). Even the hardships, the crises, and the mysteries of life are reasons for thanking God, because He makes good come from them.

This is quite pertinent to our human experience of grief. Father Solanus grasped this concept far better than most of us do when we are in the depths of darkness and despair. Not only do we resist *thanking* God, but we also do not want to admit that there is purpose for our pain. We are taciturn at times, unwilling to budge from that place of misery to which we have grown accustomed. To move beyond it and step into unknown territory with *confidence in God* seems preposterous.

If it's unthinkable to thank God before a blessing or a breakthrough, perhaps it's best to express gratitude for what we have already been given. Thinking of our blessings is incredibly powerful, particularly when we are suffocating in emotional pain or experiencing that drought of emotion from grief. We may believe it is somewhat prosaic to express gratitude for even the most basic needs God has provided for us, but once we acknowledge these, the gratitude becomes more fluid and extends to deeper, possibly miraculous, ways in which we have been blessed. Gratitude begins in the heart but encompasses the way we eventually live our daily lives. In essence, gratitude *changes* our hearts from bitterness to thanksgiving.

Once we realize what we do have, it's more credible to begin boldly expressing appreciation for what God has yet to reveal and bestow in our lives. It is precisely this act of faith that propels us into God's arms, as well as into a sphere of unforeseen beauty and richness of life. We may initially opt to make this an act of the will before it becomes an act of the soul that is deeply entrenched into every aspect of our lives.

Grief presents itself in unexpected and surprising ways, much as God presents Himself. Perhaps it is not so odd, then, to find God in the midst of our grief. When we thank Him for our pain and sorrow, as well as our joys and celebrations, we make *everything* a holy gift that He, in turn, molds into a facet of healing, strength, and peace. The turning point from unrelenting resentment to healing in the midst of our losses and even when our circumstances do not change (or, in fact, worsen) comes with understanding the gift of the cross in our holy darkness, offering God our act of conscious surrender and holy indifference to the outcome of everything, and then the magnanimous leap of trust: thanking God ahead of time, come what may.

Getting into the habit of gratitude can completely reframe our grief from an image of loss to one of potential. Some of the greatest masterpieces are born of pain and intense struggle. Perhaps God has a masterpiece in us that is waiting to emerge from our strife. When we thank Him for the sorrow, He will bless us with the gift of our grief.

From Grief to Grace

Sixth Spiritual Principle: The Wound of the Heart

"In order to live in one single act of perfect Love, I OFFER MY-SELF AS A VICTIM OF HOLOCAUST TO YOUR MERCIFUL LOVE, asking You to consume me incessantly, allowing the waves of infinite tenderness pent up within You to overflow into my soul, and that thus I may become a martyr of Your Love, O my God!"[34]

St. Thérèse of Lisieux was no stranger to grief. Death brushed her life from a very young age and throughout her adulthood. Her heart was a reservoir of purity, and her purity of heart somehow created a chasm of love that one could rightly define as white martyrdom, or a crucified heart.

The sixth, and final, pillar of spiritual development is ultimately achieving (at least minimally) the unitive state of communion with God. Although it is unlikely that we will have fully accomplished this while on earth, we may be privileged to preview glimpses of this union from time to time, depending on whether and how God chooses to reveal this to us. The focus, then, is on love of God rather than self-love. It is acquired through the deliberate desire of one's will to suffer for and with Jesus *for the sake of love* and with nothing else to gain or glean from the act of suffering. One who has entered this stage accepts and embraces all grief and pain as an opportunity to love. This is also the springboard for the love of our neighbor who is sorely afflicted with grief.

When I was a child, I was always drawn to St. Thérèse and her life story. I came to know her through my mother's affection

---

[34] This is one of my favorite quotes of St. Thérèse Lisieux from her autobiography, *A Story of a Soul* (Washington, DC: ICS Publications, 1996), 277.

and affinity for the Little Flower, and the saint's simplicity of heart and sensitivity were alluring to me. I identified with St. Thérèse's character traits, because most of the time I struggled to overcome my persistent, fiery nature. In order for me to become holy, I thought I had to conform myself to the quiet and meek dispositions of highly esteemed saints, such as Our Lady and St. Francis of Assisi.

When I learned more about St. Thérèse, however, I realized that her temperament very much mirrored my own. A sense of relief washed over me as I read stories about her tendency to cry over trite and menial grievances, as well as her struggle to accept life changes. When my mom once fondly recounted that St. Thérèse wanted to be a priest, a soldier, and a martyr, I wryly smiled to myself. I very much understood this spiritual zeal.

In many ways, St. Thérèse did accomplish all her desires and much more: her priestly calling began at her Baptism, continued in her Confirmation, and was fulfilled when she took religious vows; she became a soldier in her warrior heart, in the ways she invisibly embraced her cross in small matters and in the physical wounds of suffering tuberculosis; and she was a martyr—a mystical martyr.

White martyrdom is the long-term grief that the heart experiences for the sake of love. When we are in the thick of bereavement, the torment our hearts undergo is nearly unbearable and at times oppressive. But when we suffer these pains in union with the crucified Christ, they are no longer onerous to carry but instead become the "easy yoke" that we hand to Jesus so that He may carry them for us (cf. Matt. 11:30).

At times we are called to suffer these wounds of the heart that very much resemble physical infirmities, because Jesus is asking us to participate in His Passion for the salvation of souls. The sorrow pressing on our hearts may change from the emptiness of our personal loss to a sincere sadness for others who are hurting, wandering, wayward, and feeling forsaken. The reason for this change is that we recognize our own harrowing condition, and out of love for Jesus, we long for all lost and lonely people to unite their sorrows to His Passion as we strive to do ourselves. Our pain then becomes one with the universal grief of the Mystical Body of Christ.

When I was in college, a concept struck me for further reflection: *pain is an indicator that something needs to change.* When we are in physical pain, our bodies are signaling our brains that we need to attend to the situation before it worsens; emotional pain also triggers a similar response. Yet how often do we ignore or stifle our emotional wounds? We overcompensate for the persistent ache in our hearts by filling our lives with various distractions and diversions, ranging from superficial activities to addictions and other unhealthy behaviors. Our undying hope is that, by engaging in something far removed from the reminder of our hurts and sorrows, we might eventually be able to forget about them. Eventually we may delude ourselves into thinking they no longer exist.

Time does not always heal all wounds. In fact, time can exacerbate unhealed and unresolved pain. Pain—whether physiological, psychological, or spiritual—is God's way of grabbing our attention and directing it to the deeper, more pertinent issues that pull us away from Him. Sometimes our pain is caused by our unconfessed sins, or perhaps a betrayal we experienced without resolution and with residual unforgiveness. Our pain can be due to the void we feel from a lack of spiritual fruit in our lives. Pain, of course, can be caused by sustained sadness from losing a loved one, a job, a relationship, a pet, or because of a psychological diagnosis.

The Grace of Redemptive Suffering

Whatever the reason, pain invites us to enter into our misery and permit God to work on those unhealed wounds. Naturally, as we tend to cringe at the thought of suffering, we do not seek to penetrate our pain. Instead, we convince ourselves that we should run or hide from it, but God wants something else for us. He wants our pain to transform us. He wants our pain to teach us something greater, something our fallible senses and intellect cannot detect.

St. Thérèse knew this well. At one point, she realized she could either continue responding to her disappointments with oversensitivity from her wounded spirit, or she could allow her heart to be a place of crucifixion for the sake of love. In turn, her heart became a sanctuary that glorified God, because she handed Him her broken nature and weaknesses. She handed Him her sorrows and all that left her impoverished with emptiness and melancholy. When she consciously opted to do this, she discovered that her wounds became that gift of love, a sacrifice of self that had the power—through Divine Grace—to not only increase her own fortitude and temperance, but to also bring souls to Heaven.

When we hand Jesus our broken and bleeding hearts, He doesn't always take the anguish away from us. Instead He changes the purpose of our wounds. In the act of surrendering our brokenness and weaknesses to Him, we are giving God permission to do with us as He wills. We acknowledge everything we have covered in this chapter—our spiritual darkness, confidence that God brings about good from *all things*, and abandoning our suffering to His care. We do this in a spirit of holy indifference and out of a desire for greater humility. In handing Jesus our wounds without expectation for healing, we make a great act of love and a giant leap toward partaking in the Passion, death, and Resurrection of Christ.

From Grief to Grace

At this point, we must come to terms with what St. Thérèse herself conceded: that holy afflictions of love were preferred to feeling temporal and transitory happiness. As she did for the remainder of her earthly life, we can accept and even embrace the truth that we cannot attain the glory of resurrection without *first undergoing our own passion and death.*

God has ordained very different personal "Calvarys" for each of us. My passion is intimately tailored to my personal sanctification, which is, of course, different from yours and from St. Thérèse's or any of the saints'. The sweet surrender of giving all to God, of allowing Him to empty all the extraneous variables that hinder us from this death and ultimate spiritual rebirth, begins our journey to Heaven.

Grief can either be suffocating and spiral our hearts into a dungeon of animosity, acridity, and remorselessness, or it can be an offering of love to Jesus for as long as He permits it to continue. These are very different ways to experience grief: the source of our grief may be the same, but the potential outcomes are lived diversely. This is what separates our understanding and assimilation of suffering and loss in our lives from those who become entangled in the world's perception of trials and tribulations.

The wound of the heart is the location of our passion. It is the place where we invite Jesus to dwell, again and again, without expectations or conditions. It is by suffering *in love* that we come to a greater appreciation of and deeper love for the sacrifice that Jesus ultimately offered for our salvation. When we accept that love is incomplete without loss or death, then grief becomes beneficial and enlightening to our soul. We are more likely to embrace the various emotive dimensions of love, as well as the spiritual mysteries of suffering, death, and eventual resurrection.

St. Thérèse reminds us how God operates in a liberated and indifferent soul, a soul that is willing to undergo massive blows for the sake of love:

It is the typical method of God to come to us in unexpected ways. That is why we must expect it. The night of the Passover was known beforehand to our fathers—so that "they might have courage"—but not the particular ways that God would rescue them from their enemies.

In the Gospel, Christ is readying us for our Passover. We must be prepared, for the Lord will come when we do not expect, namely, at precisely those moments when we feel farthest from God.

Do not be afraid; be ready to open to him. Blessed are those who live expecting the unexpected. By such faith we receive the power to generate new life. As the Last Supper proves, Christ will reward our vigilance by waiting on us.

I am not at all worried about the future; I am sure God will do his will; it is the only grace I desire.[35]

Summarizing the Spiritual Concepts

How do the six principles mentioned in this chapter correlate, and what is the grand purpose for them when we are stricken with grief? In a sense, one pillar tends to reveal another until we find ourselves crashing into a spiritual supernova that illuminates everything that never made sense before.

Humility is the precursor to understanding and living out the remaining spiritual ideologies mentioned here, because it is the

---

[35] St. Thérèse of Lisieux, *A Story of a Soul*, 60.

basis for virtue development and spiritual advancement. Without it, we can be certain that our growth toward Heaven will be thwarted, but with it, all things become effortless. St. Faustina once said, "Nothing is difficult for the humble."[36]

We must pray daily for the virtue of humility, the pearl of great price (Matt. 13:45–46) that enlightens the soul toward wisdom, perseverance, faith, hope, charity, and the cardinal virtues of prudence, temperance, fortitude, and justice. Other spiritual fruits naturally bloom from humility, so we must diligently pursue it through prayer.

Humility very well may be cultivated through the dark night of the senses and soul, if that is the particular path to which God is calling you. On this journey and in light of humility, holy indifference and abandonment to Divine Providence make sense and become less onerous than before we embarked on this odyssey. Confidence in God's timing reveals the dormant gratitude we once openly expressed before our lives were shattered by loss. Gratitude, then, changes our perspective about grief, and we begin to desire to unite our wounds with the wounds of Jesus through the gift of redemptive suffering.

Humility is the basis of abandonment to Divine Providence, where we begin to focus on pleasing God rather than ourselves. Following this, we become desirous of knowing and following God's will through the principle of holy indifference. This is when we accept all consequences of situations, whether they are favorable or unfavorable to us. Our interior peace is not disturbed when misfortunes befall us. Afterward, the dark night may or may not occur, but we can all express gratitude to God for all things—that which He has already given us and that which He

---

[36] *Diary of St. Faustina*, no. 93.

will give us. Finally, when our lives are fully permeated with the sole longing to know God's will, follow it at all times, and please Him always, we love Him for love's sake and no other reason. Love then transforms our wounds of grief into an incredible gift of beauty and possibly transcendent joy.

Although it's impossible to live each one of these spiritual tenets perfectly at all times, we may try gradually to develop them. As St. John of the Cross wrote, all of life is ascent and descent. It's that interior tugging—the back and forth between our concupiscence and holiness—that draws us nearer to God. When we reach perfection, we can expect to enter Heaven shortly thereafter, for what reason would we have to remain on earth then? Let us engage the struggle with honesty and integrity. Let us remember in our interior grappling that we are weak, and our weakness is a gift that leads us to the arms of our Heavenly Father. In our weakness, we become empty, and in our emptiness, God fills us with Himself. When we grieve in this way, it becomes a thing of beauty to be admired and cherished rather than something to be abhorred.

A short reflection by Mother Agnes of Jesus, O.C.D., is the most succinct summary of these spiritual concepts when we are traversing through grief:

> There is no other secret about becoming a saint than fidelity to the grace of the present moment that gives us peace and true happiness [*abandonment to Divine Providence*]....
>
> You will become more pleasing to Jesus each day by seeing him in all things and always making your will his own [*holy indifference*].
>
> It is simple to become a saint. You have only to surrender yourself to God from moment to moment

[*abandonment*], to think of nothing but him, to pay no attention to what is not your concern [*holy indifference*], and as a result, heaven immediately enters the soul, because its emptiness attracts the fullness of God [*dark night of the soul*].

Let us climb the mountain of Love singing, knowing that pain or joy, everything that happens to us, can only increase the love of Jesus in our hearts and the peace which surpasses all understanding [*wound of the heart*].

A soul that loves God and always does his will is a world of joy for him. We should be such souls, rising by our fervent lives out of the slime of sin which covers nearly the whole earth [*redemptive suffering*].

If you have a constant desire to prove your love to Jesus, you are one of those souls completely given up to love.

The smallest act of virtue [*humility of heart*], the least sacrifice of a faithful soul under the influence of the Holy Spirit, is like a spark which escapes from the hearth and carries the fire wherever God wills. [37]

Grief is the catalyst that ignites the spark of zeal in our hearts and sets ablaze that yearning, that pining to love God wholeheartedly instead of halfheartedly. When we suffer, God adds firewood to the flame in our hearts, which both refines these six spiritual principles and extinguishes all that is not of Him. When the fire smolders into embers, He picks up the ashes and creates an entirely new masterpiece of our lives.

---

[37] "Meditation of the Day," November 19, 2015, *Magnificat* (November 2015). The commentary and emphasis are mine.

4

The Message of Divine Mercy

What is Divine Mercy? Merriam-Webster defines *mercy* as "a good or lucky fact or situation," "a fortunate circumstance," or "kind or forgiving treatment of someone who could be treated harshly," among other, similar definitions. In secular terms, these definitions suffice in most situations, but it is still limited in its scope. In many ways, mercy is synonymous with kindness and compassion, although two of the definitions here presuppose fate or destiny as the prime indicator of mercy.

Divine mercy far exceeds mere happenstance or an isolated act of forgiveness. Divine mercy is an invitation to reconciliation, peace, and healing—a bold proclamation that our redemption is from a Triune God. Divine mercy is the only means by which we can be fully restored and made whole after we have incurred grave losses. God honestly does not need to save us from our miseries. It's not His obligation, but He cannot deny us this because of love. Mercy is the way God reaches our torn and tattered hearts after betrayals and breakups. It is God's tender expression of love that is the healing balm for our open sores. Our inclination may be to run from God's invitation, and we certainly must be ready to accept whatever He wills for our personal path to healing, but divine mercy surpasses our spiritual vacancy related to grief.

The sacrament of Reconciliation is the sacrament of mercy. Growing up, I always said, "Mom, I think I need to go to Confession," and the word *confession* accurately summarized my concept of the sacrament at the time. My intention was to confess my sins and receive absolution so that I could be made clean. I suppose, while this is a very elementary understanding of the sacrament, it's not entirely untrue. Today, however, I prefer the word *Reconciliation* to *Confession* or *Penance*, as others may say. Although all are equally acceptable terms to describe the sacrament, I believe that *Reconciliation* most genuinely and fully defines the grace of *mercy* offered to us.

Reconciliation connotes conversion, because we are unquestionably altered by the healing contact of God's mercy through absolution. The *Catechism of the Catholic Church* (1424) tells us that the sacrament "imparts to the sinner the love of God who reconciles: 'Be reconciled to God' [2 Cor. 5:20]. He who lives by God's merciful love is ready to respond to the Lord's call: 'Go; first be reconciled to your brother' [Matt. 5:24]"

As a child, I avoided this sacrament, because I was reticent to admit my sins to a priest, who I believed would rashly admonish me and shamefully reduce me to the dust I was. As an adult, however, I felt God gently knocking on my heart to frequent the sacrament of Reconciliation, because I needed His restorative grace to vanquish my sins and aid me in precisely identifying them. This was an act of trust for me, because it defied everything in my nature: my tendency toward pride and resultant reticence in overcoming it.

I decided to enter into God's mercy toward the completion of Lent one year, about a week before Easter, even though I had gone to Confession about two weeks earlier. I sensed that my sins were gnawing at my heart, that somehow they were tearing me apart from the fullness of God's redemptive grace. I often reflected on how messy my interior life was as I approached the confessional, and I was overcome by the reality of my weaknesses, both petty and substantial. Fear consumed my life in nearly every direction, but I took a leap of trust as I approached the Altar of Mercy.

As I stood in line for my turn in the confessional, my eyes were unveiled with a supernatural, preeminent awareness of the grace of mercy surrounding me. I marveled at how the church was filled with penitents, both young and old and every age in between. There were entire families with young children, lone teenagers in their letter jackets, retired and widowed elderly, and single young adults. Each face carried the tenderness of God's redemptive mercy. I beheld the humility of every person there, and my heart overflowed with joy.

In those moments preceding my own confession, tears freely streamed steadily down my cheeks. Normally I would have hidden them out of shame or embarrassment, but that day I unabashedly permitted them to pour, without knowing—or caring—who saw me weeping. Part of my weeping was in gratitude for these souls who entered the sacrament with remarkable reverence, and another aspect of my tears was from personal remorse for the ingratitude with which I approached the sacrament.

These tears, it occurred to me, were sacramentals of God's mercy that He gave me that day. These healing tears conveyed the sting of my sins, but also the readiness of my heart to obtain and integrate God's love into my life. I was keenly aware that the sacrament of Reconciliation itself was an act of mercy, because it was there that all of my sinful stains were permanently washed away. Like the tears that baptized my face, absolution erased my shamefulness and restored me to the fullness of God's redemptive grace.

This is divine mercy: a sacrament, a word of absolution, tears of gratitude, and reverent reflection. Divine mercy is that invisible, ever-present grace that psychologically, spiritually, and physiologically restores us. We are made new through the waters of divine mercy, which is something mere humans are incapable of achieving. Without the presence of God's divine act of love through the sacrament of mercy, we do not completely grasp the depth of His blessing. Essentially, we are fully restored to God through divine mercy.

Extending Divine Mercy to Ourselves and to Others
"I am Love and Mercy itself. When a soul approaches Me with trust, I fill it with such an abundance of graces that it cannot contain them within itself, but radiates them to other souls."[38]

Throughout my young adult years, self-professed agnostics and atheists would muse aloud, "I'm not sure how a benevolent God would permit such horrific sufferings in this life. If such a God existed, I couldn't worship Him or follow His rules. It seems tyrannical to lord over humanity without intervening to eradicate blatant evil." This case against God never resonated with me, but I was often incapable of articulating my understanding of suffering, sin, and the plight of humanity.

Even in college, during one of my philosophy classes, we examined three points of logic that Rabbi Harold Kushner postulated about God, based on his book *When Bad Things Happen*

---

[38] *Diary of St. Faustina*, no. 1074.

to Good People.[39] He prefaced his position based on the word *when* instead of *why*. He believed that asking the question *why* bad things happen to good people was an erroneous perspective. Instead he proposed the premise that bad things do happen to all sorts of people, good and bad; therefore, the true statement should be *when* bad things happen to good people. I followed and accepted his logic until he proposed that it was impossible that God could be both omnipotent and omniscient.

We watched a film in which Kushner explained that we begin to accept suffering only when we accept that God cannot both know and be in control of everything that happens to us. I heard the rationale, and it fit the model of philosophical logic. But I could not accept this to be a morally, much less theologically, accurate appraisal.

We know that God is both omnipotent and omniscient, and yet suffering still exists. Grief is like the rain that falls on the just and the unjust (see Matt. 5:45); we know we will be showered with it at some point in our lives, to some degree or another. The Cross — our cross — is inevitable. Yet this does not negate the truth that God is still God. We weep because our human nature deeply experiences pain and suffering. Jesus Himself wept. Therefore, our suffering is not negated by our human experience but is, in fact, transformed because of it. We are capable of weeping while our hearts are simultaneously elevated to a place of hope, because we are wrapped in this cloak of mercy. Mercy acts on divine grace — that extraordinary boost we need when we are humanly incapable of believing or propelling ourselves forward.

[39] The video was of a speaking engagement that featured Rabbi Kushner in which he referenced his popular book *When Bad Things Happen to Good People*, published in 1981 by Anchor.

God is mystery—unfathomable mystery, and St. Faustina knew this intimately. We cannot begin to unravel His mind or presume to grasp the fullness of His mercy as it relates to the reality of human anguish, because His thoughts and ways are beyond ours. Yet we can trust both Tradition and Scripture. We can enter into that "abyss" or "ocean" of mercy, as Jesus described to St. Faustina.

After Sarah was born, I wrestled with this hackneyed phrase: "A benevolent God wouldn't permit His people to suffer." It taunted and enticed me to succumb to the innocuous acceptance that "it is what it is." I wondered if life were destined to be nothing more than one crisis after another, in which I meandered aimlessly in circles, no longer trying to make sense of it all, but rather numbly regurgitating the societal viewpoint that "this is all there is."

My natural disposition is to seek answers to the loftiest of questions, to pursue truth relentlessly until I have, at last, fumbled my way into a reality I could equate with my faith and reason. But no honest answers arrived after Sarah's birth. I was hurled into a chaotic state of interior confusion, and I was inconsolable. Neither my tried-and-true Catholic faith, nor people's saccharine (albeit well-intentioned) remarks allayed the torrential, internal upheaval I carried.

In the tossing and turning of my silent tantrum, I cried incessantly, "Why, God, why? Why did you allow this to happen to Sarah and to our family?" At one point, I exhausted myself from fighting the reality of our life and Sarah's rare diagnosis. I attempted to bargain, to pray for a miracle of healing, to wail and plead in desperation for the normal family I had always wanted, but God remained silent. His muted response tormented me, but I knew I had to make sense of this unexpected, maddening situation, because if I didn't, I would capitulate to resentment and interior rage.

Over time, my question *why* quietly transitioned into *what now?* I no longer asked God why this happened to us, because there was no obvious explanation that would have appeased me. I decided to enter into that abyss of His mercy, to permit Him to carry me into this unknown pit of darkness—a womb of sorts, in which I was encased in His mystery. By choosing to accept God as mystery and entering into a cryptic existential realm, I initiated the healing for which I thirsted.

It was yet another invitation to surrender my anger and anguish to a mysterious God, to experience His mercy, and subsequently to abide in His tranquility. For many months I endeavored to make sense of our situation in terms of justice, but what God asked of me was to enter into the womb of His mercy, unencumbered and undaunted by my fears of the unknown.

A beautiful poem by Rainer Maria Wilke, "Be Patient toward All That Is Unsolved" succinctly and eloquently expresses the beauty of serenely dwelling in the midst of mystery:

Be patient toward all that is unsolved
in your heart
and try to love the questions themselves.
Do not seek the answers that cannot be given you
because you would not be able to live them.
And the point is to live everything.
Live the questions now.
Perhaps you will then gradually, without noticing,
live along some distant day into the answer.

"Living the questions" is what grief looks like in action, because we have to live contentedly with the unknown and the uncertain despite our innate inclination toward comfort and ease.

It's difficult to express how God is both omniscient and omnipotent (not to mention omnipresent) while still maintaining a firm conviction that He is all-encompassing mercy and limitless love, despite the millennia of His people's toils and sorrows. A god who was not all powerful but instead possessed only limited amounts of control would not be our God. Our God knew us before we were formed in our mothers' wombs (see Jer. 1:5), and He counts every hair on our heads (see Luke 12:7). How, then, could He possess finite abilities, or be possessed at all, in fact? How could the Creator of the universe, who put the stars and planets in motion, as well as the intricate details of every wildflower in the monumental meadows blanketing the earth, be limited and unable to intervene for His creation?

How, too, could God be limited in knowledge: He who foresaw the first fall, the first sin, and consequently our inability to be united with Him for eternity without a mediator (and mediatrix)? If God knew us before we were fashioned into human bodies, how could He possibly be limited *in any way*?

This is why God is both mystery and mercy: precisely because a God who created time but is not limited by it, a God who is Creator yet remains uncreated, a God whose immensity extends beyond myself, is a God not fully revealed and yet whose face is mercy. He is, indeed, the Alpha and the Omega (see Rev. 1:8).

His mercy envelops us when we consciously opt to access it. We're certain of God's mercy, not by proving a theorem, but by allowing Him to penetrate our pain with His healing salve. When we've contemplated human suffering and the stale argument against God's goodness because of the existence of suffering, we're always pointed in the direction of mercy.

The Message of Divine Mercy

If Adam and Eve had never sinned, Jesus would never have been necessary, yet the first sin is labeled a "happy fault" in the Easter proclamation.[40] This is because *Jesus is greater than our sin*. Jesus is Mercy revealed. Jesus is Mercy Incarnate. He is the manifestation of the Father's unrestrained love for His people. We encounter mercy when we encounter Jesus.

The flow of water and blood in the image of Divine Mercy illustrates this boundless love God has for us. We delude ourselves when we emphasize sin and suffering rather than the overwhelming grace that abides with us through Jesus' total gift of self. We see this self-sacrifice when we lovingly gaze upon the Divine Mercy image, because the entire life source of Jesus—blood and water—gushed forth from His heart so that we might partake in His love. His body is a wellspring of life, and therefore a wellspring of mercy teeming for all of us. And this wellspring never runs dry, irrespective of our wounds caused by sin and strife.

His mercy is an ocean, because waves upon waves of healing are offered to us through the waters of mercy. Our grief cannot contain us if we imagine ourselves swept away by the torrential waves of love. Nothing, not our worst nightmares or most excruciating agonies, can overcome the depth and width and height of the waters of mercy.

His mercy is an abyss, because it is that ethereal mystery, that bastion of love. It is ceaseless. It enfolds us into the womb of God's love. A womb is that indwelling of darkness where we are formed and fashioned, where we are entirely vulnerable to our mother's care. The womb protects and enshrouds us from potential perils. The womb is our assurance of security. And so it is with God's mercy. It is that abyss, that womb of darkness

---

[40] "O happy fault that merited such and so great a Redeemer!"

that is mystery, that encases us so that we are infused with God's breath of life. He permeates our souls and our bodies with his healing unction of mercy.

We are graced with mercy especially in times of grief. It is when we have loved and lost, when we find ourselves facing an abysmal void, and when we are bereft with spiritual aridity that Jesus sweeps in to draw us nearer to His merciful heart. He waits for us, although He is aware of our need for temporary distance. He respects our restlessness and wrestling, our anger and fear. He expects us to lament and plead in desperation, to wail and groan as our strength shrivels and we are attenuated by our anguish.

In that weakness, we may find ourselves limping along the road to Calvary with Jesus. Somehow His Passion comes alive and has newfound meaning when we relate our own sufferings to the Cross. During the moments we reflect on Jesus' human weakness, our eyes are locked on His gaze, and we find ourselves and our pain reverberating through His torments. As St. John Paul II succinctly stated, "Redemption involves the revelation of mercy in its fullness."[41]

If the agony of Christ is not mercy, what else could mercy be? The Passion is a personification of God's mercy and love. The torture that Jesus endured transforms our sufferings and sins and all the evils we might conjure in our mind into a paradox of victory over spiritual and physical death. Suffering has its place, then, in our lives, not because God masochistically wills for us to struggle oppressively and unnecessarily, but because God became suffering as an example of what it means to overcome, to be a champion, a victor.

[41] St. John Paul II, *Dives in Misericordia* 7.

If God Himself has suffered all, then our suffering takes on an entirely different context. We no longer wallow in our narcissistic pity, selfishly whining, "Why me?" Instead, we step outside ourselves and look beyond. We capture the gaze of our Savior, and we find there not only ourselves but also Truth. We can clearly and visibly distinguish our need for Him due to our persistent hardships, and we are compelled to run to Him, despite the bloody mess of evil, loss, and struggle we know we will encounter along our life's odyssey. But we are enraptured by His love. The sacrifice He made defines mercy. To us, there is no other way to gain heaven than by losing all we know of the earth's providence and allurements.

The message of Divine Mercy extends beyond you and me into a sphere of community. When we encounter Jesus, we are inevitably and permanently changed so that our suffering is united with the plight of humanity. We then suffer in solidarity with others, whether people we know or those we may never meet in this life. Our suffering is no longer individual suffering, but is rather universal suffering. And this sense of camaraderie somehow draws us out of our selfish existence into the world in which we encounter the face of Christ in countless others who are far more distressed than we are.

We are humbled, then, by the message of Divine Mercy. Mercy first transforms us, and then we carry mercy to a hurting, wounded, broken society of people who can encounter Jesus through our lives and the way we love them.

St. Faustina wrote that "mercy is the flower of love."[42] It is also considered the sister of love. To know and extend mercy to others, we must first encounter Love Incarnate. We don't have

[42] *Diary of Saint Faustina*, no. 651.

to be particularly gifted or cognitively astute to access God's love. All we have to be is empty, open. We need to rid ourselves of the commotion and disorder that lure us away from His constant invitation and beckoning for union with Him. Once we abandon the earthly enticements that distance our hearts from His Heart, we are nearly ready to embrace our poverty of spirit and encounter the living God who doesn't just teach us about love and mercy, but who is love and mercy.

When we get to know Jesus, we cannot separate Him from the often abstract concept of love, mercy, peace, and healing. We simply know, because we first knew Him. This love changes us and makes our hearts more suited and amenable to go into the world, cast our nets into the deep, and await the encountering of those who have are spiritually adrift.

In our poverty, Jesus fills us with Himself. We are enlivened and awakened by the mystery of mercy, and we no longer require an explanation for human suffering and the existence of evil. We move beyond the existential questions that kept us caged in a suffocating and perilous oppression while we languished in our miseries. Once we encounter Jesus, however, we are at peace with the truth that not everything in this life can be known. We somehow become satisfied that some questions have no answers, that some problems have no solutions, and that some things cannot be simply reasoned away.

The only solution to our grief is to engage in a vivacious and purposeful life that is radiant with God's love. We do not gain followers of Jesus by proselytizing alone but by also choosing to live boldly in the love we have encountered. Then, and only then, are we prepared to anchor ourselves in the ocean of God's mercy and to share His wellspring with those who are marginalized.

Our grief is never experienced in isolation. What we feel is felt by God, and therefore we are capable of entering into another person's pain without it letting it become our own. We are called to do this, to be the face and the voice of the compassionate Christ, who calls us to step away from our lamentations and offer the gift of mercy to others who are stuck in their own struggles.

St. John Paul II challenges us to rethink the way we view the word *alms*. To most of us, *almsgiving* refers to donating money to worthy causes. When we do this (particularly out of our surplus rather than sustenance), we believe we are sufficiently reducing poverty. While an indirect offering to alleviate the suffering of the disenfranchised, it is an inadequate and partial means of self-giving. Our lives must ultimately exemplify Divine Mercy through the way we love others as the Holy Spirit calls us to love them — fully, without reluctance or skepticism.

Alms, in itself, must be understood essentially as the attitude of a person who perceives the need of others, who wishes to share his own property with others. Who will say that there will not always be another in need of help — spiritual in the first place — support, comfort, brotherhood, and love? The world is always too poor in love.[43]

This dearth of love is compensated in the way we view almsgiving, which must comprehensively include the gift of ourselves and possibly our livelihood rather than mere monetary handouts. Perhaps this a radical interpretation of mercy, but it certainly is a necessary one.

[43] Address of His Holiness John Paul II to the young people gathered in the Vatican Basilica, March 28, 1979.

We are not called to despair, to give up, or to give in to the inescapable losses along our life's journey. Our life is one in the Spirit. A life lived in the Triune God is a life of hope and expectancy, of earnest anticipation and resurrection. We are a resurrection people. We are a people of mercy. Let us be mercy to those without God and without hope, even and especially when we are in an unchanging state of grief.

We must recall the gift we have in suffering with meaning. Redemptive suffering connects our humanity with God's divinity. It is the surest way for us to live a life of love, because love cannot be fulfilled without suffering. To enter into this place of hope, we must regularly revisit this concept of confident anticipation mingling with pain, mercy being born from sorrow.

The Corporal and Spiritual Works of Mercy in Grief
The Corporal and Spiritual Works of Mercy beautifully apply to the topic of grief. Whether you are the one in mourning or you know someone who is, the works of mercy serve as a guidepost when we are without appropriate words to speak comfort to those in pain. While the corporal works tend to be more active, the spiritual works are just as, if not more, vital to the spiritual health of someone who is suffering a tremendous loss.

Let's outline how each work of mercy reveals God's mercy through the love we extend to others (and ourselves):

The Corporal Works of Mercy
1. *Feed the hungry:* We all know that food is not only physical nourishment but is also spiritual sustenance. When someone dies, a common gesture from many concerned people is to bring a meal to the bereaved. Although this may seem a modest token of mercy, it is actually profoundly necessary. When we are

grieving, we often neglect ourselves to the point of forgetting to eat or of not caring about food. Making a meal from scratch is too daunting a task, so we eat poorly, if at all. When a friend or neighbor drops by with a homemade meal, we are released from the pressure of maintaining normalcy in the midst of chaos, and we receive much-needed nourishment that will energize us for what we have to face. Therefore, this seemingly basic gesture of kindness is actually an enormous act of mercy.

2. *Give drink to the thirsty*: We may interpret this work of mercy literally (and it could be), but consider how those in mourning may be spiritually dry. Their wellspring of life has been emptied, and they are in dire need of replenishment. Providing them with comforting psalms or a journal may just refresh them enough to come alive again. In a crisis or a survival situation, certainly clean water cannot be overemphasized. Even when someone is waiting in the hospital for hours or days, a bottle of water may bring him or her back to the present moment and the importance of self-care.

3. *Clothe the naked*: Certainly there are situations where people are in need of clothing because of grief: a house fire (or another natural disaster), poverty, and incidental grief. Everyday essentials tend to go by the wayside when one is aggrieved, and he or she may overlook his or her children's need for winter coats and boots or even a new blanket. What a gift we can offer to others when we perceive this need and supply it through generosity.

4. *Shelter the homeless*: Perhaps someone has escaped a violent home and yet has nowhere to live. Others may temporarily be displaced because of a natural disaster or circumstantial poverty. We can respond not necessarily by opening our home as a respite for the homeless (although we may discern to do this), but

instead we can offer appropriate resources on where they may find adequate shelter.

5. *Visit the sick*: Those who are homebound often have no one with whom to converse and no one who will simply sit quietly with them. We often underestimate the profundity of visiting those who are chronically ill, hospitalized, and convalescing. Time weighs heavily upon them, but we are consumed with our busyness. If you can't think of anything material to provide for someone who is lonely, the gift of your time and presence is healing enough.

6. *Visit the imprisoned*: We seldom imagine those in prison as grief-stricken, yet many are. The vast majority of incarcerated inmates have suffered deep losses, often early in their childhoods. Some witnessed violent crimes, and many lost one or both parents. While it may be unthinkable to offer a personal visit to the imprisoned, we can find out how to participate in a prison ministry that provides greeting cards and letters to them. Letter writing can be less intimidating than entering the halls of a jail, and it also is highly valued by many who have no contact with the outside world. You can be love for the person who has never known love.

7. *Bury the dead*: How fitting for the topic of grief to bury the dead. Something so common to Western middle- and upper-class citizens may not be so accessible to others. We can help those who are unable to afford a dignified funeral and burial through financial assistance, but we can also be present with them during the ritual of burial. Burying the dead is a way of treating the body with dignity and reminds us that our souls will be joined with our glorified bodies in heaven.

The Spiritual Works of Mercy

1. *Admonish the sinner*: This is very different than proselytizing and demanding conversions from others out of our own sense of

fear for their souls. Instead, we convert the sinner through the silent but visible ways we live out our faith. We serve as living testimonies to those who are searching, and they often come to faith not by what we say, but rather by how we live. This work of mercy is the heart of the New Evangelization.

2. *Instruct the ignorant*: Some people who are grieving are unfamiliar with God's love. We can pray about how to demonstrate His love, but we must do this cautiously and over time. When grief is raw, people might not want to hear about God or His goodness, although they need Him more than ever before. Instruct them through love, and they will find God.

3. *Counsel the doubtful*: The gift of counsel can be presented in the form of empathy, reflective listening, and encouragement. More than anything else, these are ways we actively participate in someone's grief (which is both an honor and a burden). The burden can be lifted to God, who carries it on His shoulders ("My yoke is easy and my burden is light" [Matt. 11:30]), while the honor is in the gift of someone sharing his or her innermost troubles with you. Encourage with kindness and offer hope at all times, especially when despair and discouragement are evident.

4. *Comfort the sorrowful*: How appropriate to provide comfort to one in mourning. It seems obvious to do this, but few of us have mastered this delicate dance. We spend too much time focusing on our own discomfort when it's more important to allow our hearts to speak a language of their own. The heart feels what the intellect cannot always muster in words, and many times it is enough merely to hold someone's hand while he or she weeps. Spiritual comfort comes in many forms, so we must pray for the wisdom to reach people in their suffering in ways that will best help them.

5. *Bear wrongs patiently:* Sometimes the bereaved will become terse or even caustic, maybe with us. Instead of responding defensively, we can bear their anger with patience, acknowledging the raw and bitter wound that has been torn open in our presence. If we are the one offended, we can bear the suffering with patient perseverance. Either way, this work of mercy teaches us how to walk the journey to Calvary with peaceful resignation to the divine will.

6. *Forgive all injuries:* Loss can dredge up old resentments and unresolved misunderstandings. Maybe the heartbroken person longed for reconciliation, but death prevented that possibility from coming to fruition. Forgiveness paves the way to lasting healing and can occur even after someone has entered eternity. We can encourage those who never had a chance to heal those broken relationships in this life by assisting them with prayers for forgiveness or even writing letters of forgiveness. When we forgive, death and grief lose their power.

7. *Pray for the living and the dead:* When you aren't sure what someone needs when he or she has lost someone to death, send a Mass card. There are countless organizations that provide both perpetual and one-time Mass offerings for a deceased soul. Send for Mass intentions, and then deliver the card with the deceased's name to his or her family member. Not everyone will understand or appreciate this gesture, so you may want to investigate whether any of the remaining relatives are Catholic. Some non-Catholics still find comfort in this and will value your thoughtful gesture.

The Corporal and Spiritual Works of Mercy must be lived on a daily basis as we navigate how and when to respond to suffering souls. God presents limitless opportunities for us to be the healing ointment for those in need, so we must wait for the movements of the Holy Spirit to direct us to the people and situations that need the spiritual charisms we have to offer them.

His Mercy Dissolves My Misery

"There is no misery that could be a match for My mercy, neither will misery exhaust it, because as it is being granted, it increases. The soul that trusts in My mercy is most fortunate, because I myself take care of it."[44]

In many ways, my daughter Sarah embodies God's mercy. I was aghast at my first glance at Sarah. I was horrified and, I am ashamed to admit, appalled at her appearance. I immediately perceived Sarah the way the world perceives her and others like her: defective, flawed, imperfect. My eyes honed in on her mitten hands, and my interior incantation became a rhythmic plea: "Please heal her, Lord." I couldn't get past her protruding forehead and buggy eyes. It was as if every time I held Sarah, I had to face my own inability to see beyond her damaged countenance and physical features. I was both horrified and disgusted with my reaction to my own daughter.

Sarah, however, knew nothing other than the way she was molded and fashioned. Her mitten hands were always familiar to her, and she adapted rather quickly to her environment. Ben and I marveled at how she was developmentally on par with her peers in nearly every way, despite her obvious differences. In most ways, Sarah has always been a typical child, in that she sees the world through the lens of a typical toddler. She loves to be held, to interact with other children and adults, to smile and laugh without restriction or reservation. She enjoys her life and is eager to learn new skills. She is still unaware that she is

[44] *Diary of St. Faustina*, no. 1273.

not a typical toddler, which makes her innocence all the more susceptible to scrutiny and derision as she will one day certainly experience the sting of rejection and admonishment.

In other ways, Sarah amazes medical professionals as well as family members and friends. She gets frustrated, yet she perseveres. Her social skills are intrinsic manifestations of her sanguine temperament, as we have done little to teach her how to make eye contact, smile, and greet people cheerfully. She has done all this on her own and with sincere joy. In fact, she exudes joy.

I was the one in misery when God blessed me with a medically fragile child. I was the one throwing an internal temper tantrum, whining and begging for God just to make it all go away so we could have a "normal" life and blend in with the rest of society. In my misery, God handed me His mercy in the form of a naturally forgiving, joy-filled little girl who embraces life with gusto and valiantly tackles hurdles, obstacles, and challenges related to her physical differences.

Even when Sarah must undergo another surgery, she may momentarily approach the preoperative screening with trepidation, but she soon smiles and takes everything in stride. I am continually humbled by the way she handles her postoperative pain, because, while Ben and I are crumbling inside, Sarah's eyes twinkle as she greets us with "Hi, Mama and Daddy!" She cries very little and never reacts to surgeries or to her myriad appointments with specialists, doctors, and therapists as formidable drudgeries.

Sarah has already accomplished far more than most people twice or triple her age have done. And she has done so with seemingly no effort or consciousness on her part. She reveals God's mercy in so many ways, but I was blind to this truth when she was a newborn cradled in my arms. I only acknowledged what the world's voice rasped to me: that God was merciless for permitting an innocent baby to suffer life-threatening, serious surgeries and that God cruelly allowed Sarah to have a genetic mutation, which would cause her a lifetime of pain and anguish, far more than the average individual would experience.

I fallaciously accepted these unspoken cues in order to deal with the perplexity of our situation, but all in all, my misery swallowed any fragment of hope I had carried when Sarah was nestled safely in my womb. I allowed my faith to be shaken and nearly annihilated by the message of the world, which is not a message of mercy through suffering. The world's message is that of avoiding suffering, of relinquishing difficulties in order to pursue sensory pleasures and comforts. The world pities people like Sarah and even more so their families, because the world tells us that we are cruel for bringing Sarah into the world only for her to be given a dismal quality of life.

But Sarah exemplifies redemptive suffering and the hidden fortitude that rises in the midst of perceived weakness. Every day she welcomes the world with undaunted optimism, whether she is in pain from skin grafting or must take additional steps to use an eating utensil. In the face of so much visible struggle, Sarah exudes the light and love of Christ. She was born on the road to Calvary, and her entire existence is indicative of the Passion, but she carries a mystical depth, a spiritual wisdom that supplants the misery or supposed hopelessness of her syndrome.

I am captivated by her levity of spirit and demeanor. When I watch her eyes twinkle as she grins, I almost always get choked up from my own lack of faith. Looking in retrospect, I cannot fathom how I accepted the message of misery, rather than mercy, when I learned of Sarah's diagnosis. It mystifies me now, because

I am privileged to live with a child who is filled with the wonder and mystery of God. Her visible differences reveal some aspects of our Creator, who is all good and overflowing with love.

I see now that God created her exactly as she is, not because He was punishing her or our family, but rather because *He loved us so much* that He blessed us with a special child, a medical marvel, a spiritual phenom who has deeply transformed nearly every person she encountered, however briefly. I have to remember that God doesn't speak to us in powerful moments of grandeur and ostentatious drama, but instead He whispers to us in life's paradoxes, oxymorons, and idiosyncracies.

Sarah is one of the ways God has chosen to send a particular signal to the world during these times of relativism, atheism, and heresy. She isn't required to perform any miraculous acts or exhibit exemplary intelligence or talent. Her beauty, and thus God's mercy, is revealed in the virtue she bears and offers with incredible generosity to an indifferent, distant, and lukewarm society.

Sarah knows what it means to encounter people, to make eye contact and offer a healing and uplifting smile. Often that simple gesture is enough to awaken our sleepy selves, to enliven us and remind us that there is, indeed, hope still lingering somewhere within us. Sarah quite naturally and unpretentiously restores the flame of hope that has all but dwindled into quiet embers within our hearts.

This is how God chooses to speak His message of mercy in this era. We must stop having grandiose expectations of awakening through signs and wonders and instead quiet ourselves to find the hidden God, the invisible and yet profound means by which He opts to change our lives irrevocably. All of us are privy to His mercy, but we must discipline ourselves to seek solitude so that our hearts will not become drowsy and miss the blessings He presents to us in momentous ways. Solomon's canticle poetically and poignantly draws home this point: "I slept, but my heart was awake" (Song of Sol. 5:2). Let us rest in the heart of Jesus while remaining vigilant for the message of mercy He offers us.

Through Divine Mercy, our miseries are eradicated, not because God deletes suffering and trials from our lives, but because somehow those difficulties translate into a sublime implication of resurrection, and this renewal of the theological virtues carries us through each agony, loss, and torment.

The difficulty of being Catholic is that our Church isn't designed to make us feel good about ourselves. Unlike other, fluffier denominations, Catholicism seems punitive, although the disciplines of our practice teach us obedience and fidelity to God. It seems punitive, because believers are challenged on a daily basis through the rites and rituals that make our Faith rich and fulfilling. True spiritual fulfillment does not occur at the emotive or sensory level, as we have discovered. Instead of an egocentric faith, we are blessed to have a theocentric one.

Grief forces us into this stark reality, but fortunately, we can find refuge and solace in our Catholic Faith. Naturally, this is the same Faith that requires total self-annihilation, but once we have traveled along these stages of advancement for our souls, we more readily and easily recognize the truth and necessity in self-eradication and mortification. As long as we are filling the space in our hearts and souls, God has no room to dwell and rest in us.

This is why our sufferings are not automatically discarded once we delve more honestly into the fervent practice of our Faith. God may be asking us to suffer out of obedience and love for Him. He may be pruning our character through a particularly painful time. We almost always can look in recollection at our most trying moments and admit the necessity of those struggles so that we could learn a specific life lesson or grow in a virtue that we severely lacked. If we had to choose suffering, we most likely wouldn't, but we can be certain that the cross we carry is not in vain.

In essence, mercy fills the crevices of our imperfections with its perfection of love. The holes in our hearts where the world's message once existed weaken our ability both to receive and to offer God's mercy. Yet somehow, through the patience of time and His unfailing and relentless love for us, those holes are filled with His healing grace, which is Divine Mercy. I discovered that, during the times I noticed only Sarah's imperfections, I became more cognizant of my own flaws and frailties. When I looked inward, I recognized the areas of my life that desperately needed to be healed, and that is where God swept up my heart and cradled it in His loving hands, tenderly caressing the wounds and abscesses until they no longer festered with poisonous bitterness and resentment.

God's mercy completely renovates our lives as if we are new creation. As God brought the world from nonbeing into being, so His mercy is also consists in bringing a thing out of nonbeing into being. Through the gift of Sarah, God brought me out of the darkness and into His healing light.

This is the universal gift for those of us who cannot comprehend the possibility of ever exiting our place of woundedness, demise, and pain. When we are bereft because of loss, an enduring void replaces our once-contended life. It may seem impossible to believe, at least for a time, that we will ever know of life's joys and sweetness again, that we will ever smile or be made whole. But God's mercy is greater than our misery, and His gift is always available when we are ready to embark on our unique journey to healing.

Grief may disrupt our plans, but God's mercy exponentially multiplies when our miseries increase. His love overcomes our losses when we cry to Him, "Heal me, O LORD, and I shall be healed" (Jer. 17:14). What makes the onus more bearable is our promise of heaven. We know that suffering and death are not the end and that we are not prevented from obtaining this promise merely because of our life circumstances. We are given an over-abundance of joy that transcends any bodily injury, emotional or psychological burden, or even spiritual malice afflicting us. We remember that we are pilgrims on earth, and heaven is our real home, so all of our tribulations are transitory. Eternity is where paradise reigns supreme, so we look forward to our everlasting resting place in the arms of Jesus and Mary. St. John Moscatti ties in this concept with that of Divine Mercy:

Whatever happens, remember two things: God doesn't abandon anyone. The more you feel alone, neglected, scorned, unappreciated, and the more you will be near to give up under the weight of a severe injustice, the more you will feel an endless, mysterious force that will sustain you, that will make you able to have good and vigorous intentions, and you will be astonished by its strength when serenity will return. This strength is God! ...

Sick people are Jesus Christ's creatures. Many wicked people, criminals, swearers, find themselves in a hospital by God's mercy; He wants them to be saved! Nuns, doctors, and nurses that work in a hospital have a mission: cooperating with this endless mercy, helping, forgiving, and sacrificing themselves.[45]

---

[45] "Meditation of the Day," November 16, 2015, *Magnificat* (November 16, 2015).

From Grief to Grace

The more we feel forsaken, the greater is God's merciful presence and the more abundant His grace. Divine grace is exceptionally available during intense times of inner turmoil, ongoing crisis, or chronic grief. This is the fulfillment of God's promise, beginning with the fall of humanity and finalized through the sacrifice of Jesus. Mercy is our hope. Mercy is our lifeline. Mercy is the ultimate manifestation of God's love that upholds us when we are crumbling and susceptible to despair. That is why we must cling to God's continual offering of mercy. His hands are always outstretched, beckoning us to clutch them. Even an iota of longing for reprieve from the assaults of life is enough for Him to scoop us into His hands and cradle us there through the tempest. We may be on the precipice of misery, but God is our refuge of mercy.

5

Courage and Conviction:
Finding Meaning in Our Losses

"Mercy triumphs over judgment" (James 2:13).

At times the presence of grief is maddening with its silent and hidden torments. Passersby and even those closest to us do not recognize the gripping, crippling pain that erodes our ability to discover peace, much less our mission in life. Grief can mute our heart's cry to God, the one who once flourished within us and gave purpose and value to our lives. Somehow grief halts time and forces us to face the new reality of our lives. Where loss leaves a void, pain trickles in as its replacement until it overtakes our desire or capability of discovering the hidden blessing that has remained latent in the midst of our suffering.

The hidden blessing of grief, of course, is mission. Each of us is called to rise above our individual crosses, but this can be accomplished only by first entering into our pain and eventually dying to self. Grief is the beginning stage of that necessary renunciation, because it is an unwelcome visitor handing us our tailor-made crosses and inviting us to begin our journey to Calvary alongside Jesus.

Most of us aren't born with a longing for crosses or an inherent attraction to unveiling the hidden mysteries that are often dormant during times of strife and struggle in our lives. We do not masochistically hope for additional torments and agonies to afflict us. But as we advance in spiritual maturity, we begin to see with the eyes of faith rather than sensory perception. Our eyes deceive us, although we often accept optical illusions as truth when the contrary is reality.

This interior enlightenment occurs when we no longer see decay and death in the long, laborious journey to Calvary. We begin this journey reluctantly but willingly. We choose to accept our crosses after we repeatedly hear Jesus beckoning us in that subtle whisper, "Follow me." If we follow Him, we must walk with Him to His Passion (and thus our own). When we realize this, our souls are finally awakened to the truth that *mission follows pain.*

We do not pick up our crosses in a whim of naïveté, incapable of acknowledging the finality of dying to self and the eventual rising with Christ. We know the story well from annual Scripture readings of the Passion and catechesis regarding the Paschal Mystery. Despite our intellectual agreement to the profundity of Jesus' Passion, death, and Resurrection, our willingness to enter into our own passion is not immediately subsequent to this understanding.

A stark contrast exists between meditating on Jesus' Paschal Mystery and accepting our similar destiny of dying and rising with Him.

The end of the road to Calvary is evident, and the time has come for us to enter into this mystery of faith. It begins with a simple yes to Jesus' invitation of discipleship, and from there, our Lord accompanies us faithfully to the end — both literally and figuratively.

Our journey to Calvary is a life of mission. Our crosses represent the various types of grief and pain from each loss we incur. Thus, when we carry our crosses with Jesus carrying His cross, and when we remind ourselves of the marvelous outcome of this journey, our will becomes fortified and resolved to carry on—in the midst of darkness and uncertainty, despite the setbacks along the way, and especially when hope is weak and has all but vanished.

Our crosses—our grief conglomerated into one weighty, costly piece of wood—are no longer dreadful and abhorrent but are instead means to an end, which is our mission.

Each one of us is called and commissioned by God to acts of greatness. Mediocrity results from a life lived comfortably, but grief jolts us from those sensory delights. Grief shreds our comforts and pleasures into unrecognizable fragments until we are left with nothing except our emptiness, our poverty of spirit. Grief leads us to the cross of mission and purpose. Suffering itself is not the adversary; suffering is the necessity of a life that reflects greatness and magnanimity of love.

I affectionately recall a pivotal point in my journey to Calvary. My spiritual maturity hadn't yet matched my developmental age, but several movements of grief had startled me into an awakening I had never understood. I was lost. In years past, I was confident in my decisions that I was sure led me toward my particular mission in life. But all of that had changed, and I faced a restlessness of soul that was unprecedented.

As I prayed, I pondered my life and this unrevealed mission. I watched and waited with Jesus in the stillness of my heart. Silence planted the seed for contemplation, and contemplation watered that seed so that virtue would soon unfurl into delicate petals of vulnerability. I wanted those petals to face the light of the Son, to reflect God's splendor by the beauty of their simplicity and vibrancy. But I knew that seeds must be watered consistently and nourished by the Son. Only with the patience of time and gentle but firm perseverance would those seeds indeed blossom and flourish.

In a particular moment of that stillness, I felt a stirring of the Holy Spirit. I heard the whisper of Jesus in my heart, "Do you accept your cross? I want you to know that great suffering is in store for your life if you choose to accept your cross. But I will be with you, and your cross will lead you to eternal life with me in Heaven."

I was to answer this question with intentionality. The Lord, in His infinite mercy and goodness, did not want to lead me to my mission with any speck of deception or ignorance on my part.

So I was aware that accepting this beckoning would incite the unforeseen disturbances of life. I did not know what these sufferings would be, but I intuited their gravity. I also understood them to be inimitably redeeming and fruitful in ways both mysterious and exhilarating. So after careful thought and continued prayer for discernment, I felt my heart could not refuse Jesus anything He asked of me, though I did not want to suffer.

The hope of the Resurrection surged in my heart. A fire in the abyss of my soul ignited that day as I responded to Jesus with trepidation and yet with expectation of great triumph: "Yes." My tear-stained cheeks served as the first evidence of what was to be sure to test and tempt me with interminable weariness. But I could not rescind my decision. I could not refuse the One who loved me immeasurably. I knew that nothing less than my acceptance of this mystery would be an incomplete and insincere love.

"Almost always the individual enters suffering with a *typically human protest and with the question 'why,'*" Pope St. John Paul wrote in *Salvifici Doloris*. "Nevertheless, it often takes time, even a long time, for this answer to begin to be interiorly perceived. It is suffering, more than anything else, which clears the way for the grace which transforms human souls. Suffering, more than anything else, makes present in the history of humanity the powers of the Redemption."[46]

The Cross, then, is both our hope and our mission. It is our hope, because resurrection—new life—can occur only subsequent to the mystical death of self. This juxtaposition is what completes the significance of our personal path to Calvary, as well as our passion and death. To achieve our mission as Christians, we must be entirely ready to renounce our very lives in this interior death so that the promise of the resurrection—our resurrection—may be complete.

The Cross is our guidepost that redirects our focus when our lives become sidetracked. When we meander away from it, the restlessness of spirit intensifies, but when we resume our gaze upon that glorious symbol of all that we believe, all that we long for, and all that ultimately matters, our mission is actualized and activated. That is why we must continue to meditate on the Sorrowful Mysteries, to encounter Jesus in each one, and to engage our hearts to coincide with Jesus' mission.

If the Cross were nonexistent, our faith would be null. Nothing else makes sense when we try to circumvent the essence of the life of a Christian. Yet countless books, homilies, and conversations do just that: avoid the inevitable, because the Cross contradicts every existential and humanist philosophy of our postmodern era.

But the Cross, as our beacon, perhaps oddly comforts us, too. When all else becomes cognitively murky and we can no longer make sense of anything in our immediate or global surroundings,

---

[46] St. Pope John Paul II, *Salvifici Doloris* (On the Christian meaning of human suffering) 25, 26.

we look to the Cross. Somehow that momentary (or even lingering) glance redirects our thoughts, calms the fear within, and clarifies just why we continue to tarry on a road that appears to be going nowhere.

St. Faustina's vision of two paths reminds us of the value of suffering for and with Jesus and persevering to the end of life. [47] In this vision, she saw a path of lush, vibrant greenery, flowers of all varieties, and choice foods. The people on this path were exuberant: laughing, singing, and dancing while they made merry. Suddenly, they fell into a pit of fire with no warning. The distractions of worldly pleasure clouded their ability to recognize the path to perdition. The second path was worn and narrow, filled with rocks and thorns. The people along this path were weeping, bruised, and weak, barely able to continue moving forward. Some were carrying others along the way, as if they had been in battle. Then the path led to a clearing where a fine meadow greeted them, the verdant pasture of heaven. Once they entered it, they immediately forgot their sufferings.

This vision reminds us that accepting our cross and even boldly embracing it is, indeed, our mission on earth. Without the cross tailor-made for our particular means toward sanctification, we cannot be certain of redemption. Our cross is the crucible in which our redemption is contained. If we truly desire heaven, then we must learn to love our cross.

Joy Coexists with Sorrow

In my young-adult years, my mother developed a devotion to Our Lady of Sorrows. At the time, I wasn't drawn to this manifestation

---

[47] This is paraphrased from St. Faustina's vision recorded in her diary, no. 153.

of the Blessed Mother, but one comment from my mom bewildered me and yet reverberated in my mind for years: "Our Lady's joys were never without sorrow, and her sorrows were never experienced without joy."

How could it be possible to be both ecstatic and sad? Could I concurrently feel two emotional opposites? At the time, I was a counseling graduate student, so I decidedly opted to believe that this would be psychologically pathological. But, as is typical of the way the Holy Spirit speaks to me, the thought never left me. At inopportune or seemingly irrelevant times throughout my life, it often emerged in my conscious thinking.

It wasn't until Ben and I became parents, especially to Sarah, that this truth finally unfolded in a meaningful and credible manner. From the moment I gave birth to Sarah until the present moment, my heart is both afflicted with grief and uplifted with a supernatural joy. It is difficult to articulate, but essentially there is a fusion that occurred between what I mistakenly interpreted as emotive (sadness and happiness) but which is actually the supernatural gift of suffering in love and joy.

Feelings truly have little to do with acts of the will. While feelings in no way should be trivialized, they should not be the basis for spiritual self-knowledge and ultimate healing.

If I had made decisions based on my feelings after Sarah was born, I would have immediately fled the situation. My feelings were based on fear, so my very human response was to escape rather than to stay and fight. But I decided to remain, because my will overrode my emotions. My heart, distressed, sullen, and enraged, screamed from within to walk away without thought or regrets.

But I couldn't. I couldn't abandon my older daughter, my husband, and this new baby who turned out to be quite the unexpected surprise. Somehow, I shushed my heart. I didn't permanently silence it, but I asked it to simmer down for a time so that I could make a choice out of love rather than fear.

Love always asks more of us than what we feel like giving. Our visceral reactions to everyday life may be to become reclusive and deny the discomforts and challenges that we're constantly hurdling. The truth is we hate confronting difficult people, hard truths about ourselves, and unknown situations. We abhor uncertainty and struggle. We are like the rest of humanity, crestfallen and weak in the wake of battle.

Love requires more than merely conceding to our fears. All of life is one crisis or adventure waiting for us to enter, encounter, and engage. We cannot do this without divine grace. It is impossible for us to recognize that divine love relies not on our feelings but on decisions made with intentionality, much like the choice I made to say yes to God's invitation of carrying a heavier cross.

To understand this level of love requires our ability to sacrifice something we have in order to become someone we are not. In other words, we have to let go of our unhealthy attachments to what is familiar and comfortable in order to become the people God created us to be. We cannot grow without being stretched in this way, both literally and figuratively.

Consider Jesus on the Cross: His arms stretched purposefully to rouse a greater pain than what He was already enduring. His body was inconceivably expanded, and we can assume that He suffered intense agony, much as we protest when God stretches us beyond what is easy into the realm of what is cumbersome and incredibly onerous. In this way, our hearts are being stretched, but so is our character, which is being refined in virtue.

Consider this reflection by Father Jean-Nicolas Grou, S.J., that distinguishes love as sacrifice from emotive love:

The way of love is a way of faith, consequently obscure and dark; and herein consists its merit.

We walk in it blindly, not knowing where we are, and whither God is leading us. Reason understands nothing of it; and we must sacrifice it from the beginning to the end. It is but at the end of the way that we shall see the reason of the various paths along which God has made us tread.[48]

Grief does not require our permission in order for it to enter into our lives, however stealthily or dramatically. None of us welcomes grief, yet it visits all of us in a variety of ways over the course of our lives on earth. In this way, God uses grief as an impetus for us to be stretched, to grow, to become more. We must essentially surrender everything we have come to know and love and to which we have attached ourselves in order that fortitude may be cultivated in us. This is how our offering of suffering to God becomes malleable in His hands, although we may never fully recognize the spiritual results in this life.

We come to the realization that joy is unrelated to our fleeting, existential moments of happiness when we process our own experiences of grief. Happiness becomes a very superficial moniker, and we altogether eliminate it from our vocabulary. We no longer seek to "be happy" or for our children to "live happy lives," because we know that is rather impossible. We know their lives will be filled with unforeseen tragedy, betrayal, heartbreak, and sorrow.

Yet sorrow is the crucible of joy. If we permit God to enter into our wounds, and we trust Him wholeheartedly, we find that

---

[48] "Meditation of the Day," March 26, 2015, *Magnificat* (March 2015).

sorrow contains inexplicable, inexpressible joy. Joy elevates our hearts to the heights of heaven. We are able to soar above the mere experience of suffering when joy permanently resides in our hearts. At times, we are capable of losing sight of the suffering altogether when we are enraptured in God's love.

His love is what has transformed our lives of chronic grief and one unexpected debacle after another. Joy is the fruit of a soul refined in His love through the vessel of suffering.

Joy and sorrow comingle in our hearts at any given moment. There are times when we casually converse with strangers or even engage in lively dialogue with our spouses or friends, and sorrow may surface just as frequently as joy does. We are never truly prepared as to when or how we might be pierced with the sword of sorrow or the lance of joy.

Sorrow is ever present for me, because I am the primary caregiver of a medically fragile child. My lifestyle differs greatly from mainstream moms with children of the same ages as mine. Sorrow enters when I do not know how to relate to other mothers on a substantive basis, and shallow conversation leaves me unfulfilled.

Yet joy also lingers in my soul, despite the daily struggles and draining medical appointments. Joy rushes through my heart when I notice my daughters offer a spontaneous prayer of gratitude to God, because "He made all the flowers, Mama." Joy hoists our spirits when we receive a small, handwritten note from a friend, read an inspirational quote from Scripture or a saint, hear an encouraging song, or receive a smile from a stranger. Joy is packaged in all sorts of praises and people. It is simply more difficult to notice joy when we are in the throes of grief.

Suffering has a way of leading us down the treacherous path of despondency, which easily ends in despair. The enemy clutches at every opportunity to manipulate our grief so that we become discouraged and focused narrowly on ourselves. But God wants us to offer Him our grief so that we are equipped to step outside of our difficulties and discover healing by reaching other people with the spiritual gifts and natural talents we have to offer.

God may not eradicate the source of our grief or even extend physical healing if we or our loved ones are chronically ill. Instead, He may approach you as He did to me: "Do you accept your cross? Yes, life will be hard, and it will hurt. But you will make your mark on the world. If you put your hand in mine, we will accomplish great things together."

Would you rather leave a positive legacy or unresolved resentment when you die? Grief is the crossroads where we pause, give consideration to our options in light of our faith and in the raw concupiscence of our human struggle, and make our decision for hope or haplessness. What we select irrevocably implicates how we are changed and become change agents for a hurting world.

Reveal and Heal: The Gift of Authenticity

When I was a child, I was often reprimanded for my loose tongue. Naturally, I suppressed many thoughts and emotions, not out to prudence and temperance, but out of shame and fear. Truthfully, I was a crass and brassy youth. I didn't think before I spoke, and I allowed my heart free rein over my speech. It wasn't until I was a young adult that I realized the many wounds I created due to my abrasive words, and I began praying for wisdom to exhibit self-control over how, when, and what I spoke.

I still struggle with careful and reflective responses to topics or personal admonishments that evoke intense emotions in my heart. The difficulty in maintaining silence when I would rather defend myself or put someone in his or her place absolutely makes my cross heavier, and although my ego is not spared from humiliation, that same humiliation fortifies the virtue of humility.

Some people, on the other hand, are so guarded that it is nearly impossible to decipher their personal beliefs and convictions, let alone their feelings. Their defense mechanism is one of safety, so that their hearts may not become crushed by dissension when others choose to opine on hot-button issues.

Where is the point of moderation between uncharitable speech and fear of emotional intimacy? Is it feasible to maintain our authenticity without always speaking our minds? On the other hand, we may fruitlessly hope to foster friendships with others who remain unwilling to share their hearts with unapologetic honesty.

Grief seems to trigger our natural inclinations toward safety as a result of hypersensitivity or toward brazen, spiteful language as a result of rising anger. Yet God wants to reveal His love in and through us so that He may be able to heal our wounded hearts. Because grief involves negative and difficult emotions, we may not welcome the opportunity for vulnerability to others. Emotional transparency certainly has its risks, particularly during such a fragile time in our lives as when we have experienced loss. The negative feelings are uncomfortable, awkward, and unfamiliar to some of us as well, so we aren't always certain how to process and express them in a healthy manner. The problem with both silencing and exploding grievous emotions is that we are inadvertently (or possibly consciously) building emotional barricades around our hearts so that we might prevent further heartbreak and strife from wounding us.

Grief cannot be silenced. Even if it is not overtly verbalized, it remains festering until we welcome it and ask ourselves the tough questions surrounding these difficult emotions, such as guilt, fear, anxiety, anger, or despondency. These feelings may be triggered spontaneously or exacerbated during milestones, such as the first anniversary of our loved one's death or a special holiday, such as Mother's Day. If we do not express these negative emotions initially, then we will internalize them until they swell into anger.

Uncontrolled or repressed anger may be expressed as wrath or indignation and is often hurled at unsuspecting, innocent people. Projection of anger occurs when someone innocently remarks about something seemingly mundane or maybe even brings levity to a situation, but these comments remind us of our pain, so we snap in an unacceptable and inappropriate way. Fury that is expressed uncontrollably often displays itself as verbal aggression or abuse. When this occurs, clearly our anger has become sinful, and we must learn healthy ways to channel that anger without hurting another person.

Father Simon Tugwell, O.P., offers a poignant suggestion on how to overcome sinful anger:

> We think that we are entitled to be annoyed at somebody. If we succumb to this, then we shall devote our attention to the thought of the person with whom we are annoyed. What the ascetic needs to do is focus his attention instead on the fact that he is annoyed. Instead of seeing some other human being angrily, he tries to see his own anger. He can then begin to fight against it.
>
> We need to reclaim anger for its proper purpose. It is always a waste of good anger to get annoyed with other

human beings. Instead we should turn our anger precisely against our thoughts ad against the demons who deploy them.

In this way we shall be using anger in accordance with its true nature, to clear a way through the thoughts which swarm all around us, so that we can gradually come to a clearer perception of what it is all about. Thus we move from a fairly blind lashing out against whatever seems to be getting in our way to a position where we are fighting in the daylight.

The desired goal of this whole exercise is a state in which we are no longer at the mercy of inappropriate reactions. And this is a profound state of balance and harmony.[49]

In essence, we must redirect our thoughts from the person who may have provoked our anger to the anger itself. This brings about emotional and spiritual maturity through introspection, so that we are better equipped to quiet and reframe our negative emotions before they become completely out of control.

Here is a theorem of anger as a simplified depiction of the potential for sin or virtue, depending on our response to anger:

Anger (seed) → fury/rage (acts of violence through speech or physical altercations; and internalizations of isolation and neglect of relationships) → bitterness (the fruit)

Persecution/slander/victim of anger (the seed) → resentment (the fruit)

---

[49] "Meditation of the Day," November 20, 2015, *Magnificat* (November 2015).

God wants to intercede in this way:

Anger or persecution (the seed) → divine grace (spiritual stimulus) → the sacraments (food/nourishment) → mercy/peace/joy/love (the fruit).

God doesn't want us to become victims of sinful anger; rather, He longs to intervene in a miraculous way so that our intense negative emotions can be soothed through His grace.

Other negative feelings that tend to be associated with grief include guilt, sadness, and despondency. All of these can oppress us if they are ignored or improperly expressed. However, unlike anger, the remaining three common negative feelings tend to be internalized rather than outwardly verbalized or demonstrated to others. Of these, guilt may lead to unhealthy and harsh self-punishment, while despondency may descend into outright despair. Naturally, the enemy preys on these weaknesses, since we are more susceptible to them during our vulnerability and sensitive state of grief.

Negative emotions, while they may be intense and reveal our discomfort, are not sinful in and of themselves. They become impediments to our spiritual growth, because we have effectively shut out other people and possibly God through our inability to share our feelings or our hostility toward others authentically. A fairly simple and straightforward method of harnessing negative emotions related to grief is by keeping a journal. Merely recording our thoughts and reactions in writing spurs greater self-awareness and appropriate emotional intimacy with others.

God cannot operate without restraint in us when we are creating tidal waves of hostility in our relationships, nor can He even reach us with His grace when we remain closed due to our paralyzing fears. We must approach Him with sincerity of heart, a true desire to change, and this requires unabashed humility. We begin by asking for the grace to grow in the virtue of humility, and then augment that resolve through frequenting the sacraments of healing: Reconciliation and the Eucharist.

Over time, we will recognize God's gentle beckoning. Our anger loses its jagged edges around our hearts and becomes softened with the gift of charity. We are no longer inclined to respond to people's comments in conversation out of impulsive ire, or we may find that the barricades we have built to protect our hearts begin slowly to crumble until they are one day nonexistent. This is how God reveals a healthy and holy authenticity within us so that we can touch other people's lives in such a way that both we and they are healed.

Healing does not occur in isolation. We cannot hole ourselves up, waiting for an end to our suffering and strife. Conversely, we cannot fight our way through life, subconsciously maligning others so that they may writhe in the same level of pain that we do. Only when we let go of the invisible rivals we've conjured in the midst of our grieving can God's work take place subtly and steadily erode the unhealthy and unholy darkness we've permitted to fuel our response to life.

Holy authenticity is a charitable candidness in both heart and soul. The operative word is *charitable*, because, as noted, it is possible to be entirely transparent to others without demonstrating concern for others. So God may draw us inward for a time, excavating the source of our angry outbursts so that they may be tempered with the flame of kindness. But growing in charitable authenticity may mean that others are drawn out of themselves and their community of isolation so that they may begin to share their opinions and feelings with honesty and ease.

Achieving authenticity involves frustration and failure in order for spiritual and emotional growth to take place. Healing often progresses with the revelation of God's gentle persuasion as His grace and gifts overcome our sorrow. The mention of specific spiritual gifts or acts of divine grace is purposefully excluded, because God bestows different types and degrees of these gifts on everyone, depending on need.

We must never forget that God's grace compensates for our lack. Our greatest weaknesses can serve Him just as much as our natural fortes can. In fact, God often uses the areas in our lives that cause the most struggles for us to manifest Himself in and through us. This perpetuates a fluid cycle of humility, so that we can never truly take credit for some act of greatness that befalls us. We must honestly admit with immense gratitude that it is truly God who reveals and heals in and through us.

Where do we go from here? How do we make sense of our particular mission that has possibly been hiding in the wounds of our grief? Mission is very rarely unmasked overnight, as with St. Paul's dramatic conversion on the road to Damascus. Instead, mission progresses in a series of patterns that God makes known to us as He heals our grief-stricken hearts, much as He did when the scales fell out of St. Paul's eyes. The scales are the ways in which we have become accustomed to living after we incur arcane losses.

Grief may be cryptic to us and cloud our interior vision with the scales of esoteric suffering, but God longs to reveal His truth to us, which is enveloped in the gentle healing that reveals our stubbornness, our weakness, our wrestling, and our agony.

None of life is lost on God. All that we undergo plays a vital role in the story of our lives. We cannot go forth to change the world until we, ourselves, have been entirely transformed by His placid coaxing to give all that we have been, all that we are, and all that we will become into His care. Ultimately, revelation and healing give birth to mission, and our mission is the trajectory of the rest of our lives. As St. John of the Cross so aptly summarizes, "In the eve of life, we will be judged on love." Let us choose love, then, to override our fears. Let love be our guide, our mentor, our revealer, and our healer. Let love be all in all in and through us. And in the end, love will then prevail in and through us.

Epilogue

Chances are, you have read this book because you recognized the tiny flicker of hope in your soul, despite your hardships and defeats. Chances are, you opened the pages, because you were ready to embark on an expedition not only of self-discovery but, more importantly, of spiritual enlightenment. We all traverse many roads, but the Church is our beacon and refuge in times of uncertainty and incomprehensible confusion. She illuminates the steps before us so that we walk with a particular confidence. The cadence of our stride may, at times, be weak, but it is a rhythm of hope that synchronizes with the rhythm of love in our hearts.

When I first uttered that prayer to God as a little girl, "I want to do great things for You, Lord," I never fathomed that I would find my calling in the midst of tragedy. The palpable tension that grief often leaves in its wake (literally at times) doesn't seem opportune for regrowth and rebirth. Instead, grief is rife with raw agony and emotional torments. Who are we in the midst of unthinkable suffering? Likewise, who is God, and where can He possibly be?

God often seems to be hiding when we are seemingly drowning in the torrents of our fears. When we are shaken inside by some unforeseen and certainly unwelcome guest of grief, the emptiness in our hearts is too overbearing for a time. It is too insurmountable to carry grief without acknowledging its presence. Even when we openly admit the gaping wound that loss left behind in the place of a dream, a person, a relationship, or a job, the pain itself does not subside.

It is only when we consciously enter into our pain that the journey to healing begins to materialize that latent mission that we were incapable of seeing while mourning in darkness. Perhaps we remain in darkness, but once we take God's hand and proclaim our wholehearted yes to His mystery—without apprehension or regret— He unveils our calling within the black hole of sorrow. We begin to realize it was there all along.

Not long ago, I was reflecting on my life and deciphering particular patterns that seem to have led me to where I am today. Not only did I develop a passion for writing and inspiring others from a young age, but I also see how God permitted very specific occurrences to influence and challenge me so that I might be ready for the task to which I am currently involved: writing, coaching, and reaching countless people through the message of triumph over tragedy.

Somehow the conviction He laid upon my heart never cooled its embers, although at times they were quiet and fading. My heart always burned with an earnest fervor and ardor for God, but I often suppressed it due to the continual presence of fear. Would it surprise you, dear reader, to know that I face incalculable fears every day? I am afraid of almost anything you could muster in your imagination, both real and perceived fears (i.e., phobias).

But God's grace has mastered my fears, and it began with my yes in the midst of the wrestling and bewilderment following Sarah's birth. That yes was what I considered at the time to be a very miniscule and meager act of capitulation, yet it was that weak yes—not fully understanding what lay ahead and not entirely empty of trepidation—that thrust me into my mission. God waited for that act of faith, however faltering it was at the time, and transformed it into a greater act of trust along the way.

Mission is often born of tension. We cannot possibly know or even care to know what our purpose on this earth is while we remain complacent and comfortable. If we live for ourselves, we may very well never truly awaken to our mission. But if we sincerely seek, through prayer and discernment, what God has called us to do and created us to be, He will most assuredly answer that question. But it may not be in the form we would hope, in some grandiose act of success or renown. Instead, it most likely will mimic the pattern of saints throughout the ages: a tragedy followed by an awakening and, finally, conversion.

Mission tends to gradually unfold and without drama or splendor. It seems that the Holy Spirit most often works by placing bits and pieces of a grand puzzle together that form the full image only when our lives are complete. As I have, you may look in retrospect on your life and notice emerging patterns that have led you to be the person you most long to be in this life. These are the two or three pieces of a puzzle that God so intricately interlocks. We may be privy to glimpses of what that image may become one day, but very seldom are we privileged to see our mission in its entirety, as in the form of prophecy.

God purposefully unfolds our calling with delicacy and deliberation in order that we may not waver from trusting Him and clinging to Him in childlike dependency along the way. Certainly there will be terrifying moments, as well as enlivening opportunities, as our mission unfolds. But each step reaffirms our original yes to God when we were still lost and alone in the darkness of uncertainty and sorrow. Each step subsequently offers us a new challenge that, should we persevere, will immensely grow our character and our resolve to do great things for God.

As I write this, my heart burns to glorify God with every word I write and speak, but I consider myself to be very ordinary. In fact, my life most likely resembles yours in very typical ways. I live in a sleepy rural town nestled in north-central Indiana, where Catholicism is not only unusual but is also repelling to most of the fundamentalist Anabaptists in our area. I shop at Goodwill for our clothing. I have secondhand furniture. And if you stop by unannounced, I will greet you with a smile (and possibly soiled hands from either cooking or changing a diaper) and invite you inside for an impromptu chat.

But what sets me apart from you? Quite simply, my mission is unique to my gifts, talents, virtues, and life experience. Your mission is one that only you can present as your gift to the world and ultimately to God. Neither of us can replace the other. That is why I hope you close this book with your heart elevated to the heights of heaven, resounding in joyful expectation that God is calling you to greatness.

I leave you now with a summarizing thought that I hope lingers in your soul for a time so that you may ponder its meaning for you where you are now in your life. Don't succumb to the wiles of the enemy, who would rather that you interminably wallow in your grief. Don't cave to the worldly temptation that suffering is meritless and should be avoided. Instead, rise up and offer your wounds to God as an act of trust and love. Your gift is the first step in unraveling the beautiful petals of your mission to change the world from apathy and mediocrity into one that is set ablaze with charity, hope, and the renewal of faith.

Epilogue

Joy and woe are woven fine,
A clothing for the soul divine;
Under every grief and pine
Runs a joy with silken twine.
It is right it should be so,
Man was made for joy and woe;
And when this we rightly know,
Through the world we safely go.[50]

---

[50] William Blake, "Auguries of Innocence."

Appendices

Appendix A

A Father Reflects on Grief and Suffering

My husband, Ben, and I were discussing our respective encounters with grief, and we agreed that men and women most likely process and express grief quite differently. Furthermore, we reflected on how men in our Western society often receive indirect (or overt) messages that it's unacceptable for them to convey intense emotions, particularly negative ones. In turn, men may struggle in recognizing the prevalence of grief when it becomes evident after a period of latency. This reflection is an offering from my husband's heart to the hearts of grieving men everywhere so that they may feel indirectly permitted to share their own sorrows and struggles.

There are few moments that I can recall in my life that have had massive impacts: graduating from college is certainly one, and marriage is another (and certainly greater) event. The birth of my first daughter ranks up there as an impacting experience, too, but these are all happy occasions, and one would expect a happy occasion to bring joy to the heart. Not all experiences that have a lasting impact are necessarily happy, but rather, some suddenly become shocking, because they have changed your life and your worldview forever. For me, such an event was the birth of my daughter Sarah.

It was March, and I remember the weather being windy and cold with freezing rain. Jeannie had given pretty solid indications that she was going into labor, and I felt happy and confident about the whole process. We had done it once before, and going to the hospital was easy for me. Thinking of the first time I would meet this little girl and the future we would share together as a family was something that warmed my soul and brought praise to God, who knitted this little girl in Jeannie's womb. The labor progressed fairly normally, but when it was time for delivery, this stubborn little girl just wouldn't come out.

I was slightly puzzled by this, since everything from our sonograms showed a normal little girl. I was tired at this point, but certainly nowhere near as exhausted as Jeannie, who had been in labor for twenty-four-plus hours. The news came that a cesarean was necessary, and Jeannie was devastated, since that is what she had been dreading. In the back of my mind there was a nagging feeling that something was not right, but I held back those thoughts, because I knew that Jeannie was counting on me to be a source of strength when sleep and worry made it seem as if her world were falling apart.

Once she was wheeled into the operating room, I soon followed and sat beside where her head rested. I honestly wanted to watch the operation, but I knew that if I did, I would blurt out to her what was going on, and I don't think that would have been appreciated at that moment. Hormones, sleeplessness, and anxiousness can do bizarre things. The operation went beautifully, but it was after this moment when my world fell apart. The last ounce of strength I was holding on to was now held by God's grace alone.

I saw her. I saw her hands, her feet, and her poor squished nose and brow. I knew something wasn't right, and I was now standing on the precipice of my own little bubble being popped unceremoniously. Something was wrong with Sarah. She screamed like a newborn, but she didn't look like one to me. Her webbed toes, mitten hands, and pronounced brow had suddenly become hard to look at, yet, once again through God's grace, I was able to open my heart and arms to her.

The selfish, egotistical side of me was suddenly at war with the humble and providence-seeking side. It felt like two armies at fever pitch when they had just clashed swords against shields in a swirl of action. God had knocked the wind out of me, and ike a slender glass vase that has shattered into a million pieces, I never thought I would be put back together.

In the years since her birth there have been many questions and many trials. God has asked me to sacrifice a lot, but in so doing He has turned the meager amount of bread and fish I can offer into great blessings. Sarah has come through her surgeries and challenges with a joyful heart and courage beyond measure. This tiny child has taught me more about sacrifice than anyone I have known. She goes through it all with a smile.

At times it's difficult to bear those initial thoughts that I've been plagued with since her birth: thoughts that she would have been better off if she had quietly passed away after birth or through miscarriage, thoughts that we would all feel guilty about having because they put our selfishness squarely into focus. I see the providence now in this little girl. Her large blue eyes staring back at me in an adoring manner melt my heart and help me come to grips with my first thoughts about her. This little soul will grab your heart and never let go. She will shake you from your little world and make you question what you see. She forces everyone to view her soul and not her perceived defects. This is how she has transformed my life.

It is easy to have your eye drawn to physical beauty but most difficult to look at those who do not meet the worldly definition of beauty. Once you spend any time with Sarah, however, those thoughts quickly fade, and you cannot help but look for the soul in each person. You seek the human soul, because you question what the world values. You begin to strip away the exterior and look for the interior.

Many times we as fathers leave the emotional aspect to the mothers to talk about and relate to others. We just listen and nod and grunt in approval while so many other thoughts that are left unsaid are never verbalized. I suppose in some way we are built to be involved in action. Work, play, building, fixing, mowing, or any of the numerous tasks that fill our day are meant to be ones of action. Contemplating and beginning to come to grips with those things that devastate our little world are not always things that we can verbalize. This must change.

God is always calling us to action, but many times those actions are not what we think. The action of contemplation, of moving beyond the superficial is critical and will help us to be better fathers. Prayer, and lots of it, will help us through this world of contemplation and bring us back to the arms of Jesus.

Through all of this and beyond the initial shock of Sarah's birth, I have been able to reflect upon being a man in a situation that has great emotional weight to it. Most men respond with detachment, burying themselves into their work, losing themselves in promiscuity, drugs, drinking, or any other number of dead ends. This is not to say all men fall into these traps, but the temptations are always present, offering the false promise of relief from the grief that they feel deep in their heart.

Depending on your family of origin, there's the possibility that grief was never allowed to be shown in the form of crying or any other manner that would, in turn, push you into self-destructive behavior. Men honestly do not receive any societal cues on what is an appropriate way to express grief. We tend to see two extremes: the man who has fallen apart into a blubbering mess and the man with a stiff upper lip who does not let on about the devastation inside. Neither is healthy, and neither really strikes at the root of the problem. Men need outlets for the swirling storm of grief away from societal and family pressures.

Women tend naturally to express their emotions outwardly, and men tend to channel their emotions through an activity or let those emotions spill into daily responsibilities. If you're angry with your wife, that anger tends to get directed at employees, drivers on the road, or others who may be unwitting targets. This is where men should begin to recognize patterns in their daily actions to find how grief is expressing itself in their life. Are you numbing your pain through some diversion so as to avoid the grief? Are you angry at the situation that there's nothing you can do about? Are you devastated that your life plans have come crashing in, yet you still pursue avenues that aren't possible to achieve? Just be honest with yourself, since that is the moment you'll begin to move toward healing your grief.

Balancing the emotion and the response is key to walking on this tight rope of grief. The strength of the emotion should be tempered with an appropriate response in an environment that is open and welcoming. The best example I can give is that I take a yearly camping trip in the spring. I go with my closest friends, and the days are spent hiking, canoeing, hanging around the campfire, and just taking a much-needed break from the rushed pace of life. In this environment we all have a chance to expend our energy in various activities throughout the day and withdraw from the pressures of family life.

There is a cursory moment where we sit in front of the fire and begin to let our guard down. It doesn't have to involve long explanations of our exhaustion or relentless sobbing; it is just a short, raw moment in which the cathartic statement is complete. Affirmation is expressed from the rest of the guys, and we've had our moment. Nothing needs to be solved or fixed. Just that raw moment is enough for most guys to get it off their chest and relieve that burden. Just as Confession allows us to let all of sin off of our shoulders, so do these moments allow for grief to be stripped from our heart.

Not everyone has an opportunity for "campfire catharsis," but there are other avenues for men to share in their grief. A trusted friend should certainly be consulted. A pastor or a priest would be another wonderful resource for spiritual direction, since grief has a deep spiritual connection. (Think of Christ in the garden of Gethsemane.)

Whatever the avenue, the grief should be shared with another man. This is not because women are incapable of helping men process painful emotions, but at the core of a man is the need for an affirming response from another man. Just as we wish to please our fathers when we are children, so too does the need come into our hearts when we are in immense grief to have our heavenly Father affirm us through another man on earth. Prayer, contemplation, and the recognition of the struggle are also key components that need to be placed in some way in our daily lives. Pray for God's grace, contemplate your journey and how you take each step through the dark forest of grief, and recognize that there will be struggles and setbacks that take you to places you've never been before.

The process for men to process grief is very simple but intense: recognize and accept the grief, and be affirmed by another man in moving past your pain. This process could certainly take a long time, since we tend to busy ourselves with many other tasks while putting off the one activity that can help bring about a real change in our lives. Another obstacle you may encounter is finding the affirming male figure you need. There may seem to be a shortage of male role models in our culture, but you may find them in very unlikely places.

Once a man recognizes that life—and grief—is an adventure and a process, he can begin to heal with God's grace.

Appendix B

Meditations on the Stations of the Cross, the Sorrowful Mysteries, and the Seven Sorrows of Mary

The following meditations on the Stations of the Cross, the Sorrowful Mysteries of the Rosary, and the Seven Sorrows of Mary invite you further to contemplate and reflect on how redemptive suffering specifically pertains to your experience with grief. Merely reciting these meditations will not suffice to deepen your appreciation for the summons to a greater love through suffering. When the meaning of sacrifice becomes more evident through this walk with Jesus and our Lady, our own blunted grief softens into gratitude and charity.

Seize the quiet moments that invite you to solitude and contemplation. Your thoughts will undulate into prayers, which will be solely motivated by increased ardor and devotion to the infinite God, who reaches into your heart and resides within the crevices, fragments, and wounds. So read these meditations in a setting conducive to prayer, as they are written in the form of both a prayer and a reflection, from your heart to the united hearts of Jesus and Mary. Imagine yourself as the subject of each meditation so that it may become intimately personal for your walk with Jesus.

Prayer before Personal Meditation[51]

My God, I firmly believe that You are here present, and I humbly adore You in union with the angels and saints. I am sorry for having sinned, because You are infinitely good and sin displeases You.

I love You above all things and with my whole heart. I offer You all that I am and all that I have, my soul with all its faculties, my body with all its senses.

Enlighten my understanding and inflame my will, that I may know and do what is pleasing to You. I beseech You to direct all the powers of my soul, all my thoughts and affections to Your service and Your glory as well as to my own sanctification and salvation.

---

[51] "Prayer before Meditation, Study, or Spiritual Reading" Catholic.org, accessed November 22, 2015, http://www.catholic.org/prayers/prayer.php?p=2060.

Meditations

The Stations of the Cross

First Station: Jesus Is Condemned to Death

I marvel at the impossibility of Your condemnation. You are my God, my only Savior, and yet You have been marked for death? It cannot be so. In my denial, I ignore the unfolding scene that leaves me with more questions than answers. Life isn't supposed to end this way, is it? The just man suffers an abominable death, while the sinner is released. But it's true, and the reality stuns me into silence as I quietly slip away from the mob of accusers. Surely it is not I, Lord, who has brought You to such a time as this.

Second Station: Jesus Takes Up His Cross

As if the astonishment never ceases, I observe an even more puzzling moment: You accept the Cross that is handed to You. Why don't You flee, Jesus? You are more than capable of it. Why not run away from Your certain demise? It's clear that things will only worsen if You stay the course, so I wait for You to change your mind and walk away or miraculously end this charade. But it doesn't happen, and I cannot understand how and why You would voluntarily lead your faithful to such slaughter.

Third Station: Jesus Falls the First Time

As Your body collides with earth, the dust fills my eyes, and I am temporarily blinded. Yet in my impaired vision, the eyes of my heart are illuminated. You are the light I see in this moment. You are my light, my only hope. Is it true that my only hope can be discovered on the road to Calvary? All that I have ever known to be true is being contradicted as Your weakness reveals mine. It is strength I see in You, Jesus, not limitation, and I know that my destiny must imitate Yours on this day. You are preparing my heart for my own spiritual anguish, but I cling to Your promises. I know You will not fail me.

Fourth Station: Jesus Meets His Sorrowful Mother

My Lady, my Mother, how can your heart carry on while your only Son's death is prolonged by torment and torture? Your heart bleeds with His, and I see the union you share — one of breadth that exceeds any blending of hearts I have ever seen. All at once, my soul is elevated to a place of aching for that union, a total union of unspoken love. Is this love? Is love this ugly and dark? How can the Father allow such a tragedy? Show me, dear Lady, the way to Heaven, for where you go, I know your Son also is.

Fifth Station: Simon of Cyrene Helps Jesus Carry the Cross

As Simon of Cyrene fumbles with the Cross, I secretly admire him and yet am equally relieved it was not I who was asked. The day wears on, and my body grows weary with physical exhaustion and emotional depletion. When will this end? A quick, sure death seems more benevolent than the severity and cruelty of crucifixion. Why does sacrifice entail so much bloodshed? I wonder if I will be exempt from this or if Jesus will expect me to follow in Your footsteps. Something stirs in my heart, a delicate nudge, and I know I must do the same. Even if I do not die on a cross, I must help You carry Yours. Simon has shown mercy, and I am called to do the same.

Sixth Station: Veronica Wipes the Face of Jesus

Veronica's love for You shames my cowardice. I have stood on the sidelines so far, merely observing as if entertained by an amusing performance. Veronica's courage to stand out among the raging crowd reminds me that love does not ask *why*. It simply accepts what is required and is content to respond, to encounter. Veronica is encountering You, but I falter in my devotion. Where am I in this darkness? Where do I belong?

Seventh Station: Jesus Falls a Second Time
Alhough I initially clung to the hope that the end of this madness might come quickly, that hope has faded, and my heart is left bereft with despondency. I do not want to despair. But nothing in these events looks brighter than bleak. I feign a smile as a few of Your disciples brush past me, but inside I, too, am dying alongside You, Jesus. Where is the fulfillment of the promise? I imagined You renewed in strength after Your first fall, but instead Your weakness mortifies and confounds me. I know I am selfish for wanting this pain to be over, but I've never experienced something so horrific, especially to my Lord and God. Save me, Jesus, in Your fall. When I fall, I will remember this moment and pray for the courage to rise again, despite my anguish.

Eighth Station: Jesus Meets the Women of Jerusalem
It gladdens me to see several women consoling Your heart, Jesus. It seems as if their presence boosted Your resolve to carry on to the bitter end of it all. I still do not want to watch You die on a Cross. Such a crude piece of wood cannot be the means of extinguishing such an almighty God. Or is my pride blinding my ability to see the beauty, the gift of Your sacrifice? The women of Jerusalem see it, Jesus, and their gratitude is expressed through their encouraging words and kind gestures of love that sustain and even rejuvenate You. I want that kind of determination, but I am sorely lacking in virtue. My nothingness grips me, and once again, I turn away in shame.

From Grief to Grace

Ninth Station: Jesus Falls the Third Time

I can no longer bear to see you fall under the weight of the Cross. The King of kings, Lord of lords, and Priest of priests should never be the object of such a humiliating spectacle. I imagined You on a throne, sovereign and majestic, not nearly naked and stripped of even flesh. In Your weakness, save me, Jesus. In Your weakness, lift me up. I cannot stand here without You, for when I fall, it will be to sin. In You there is no darkness, athough everything encircling me is black and drear. I hope in You alone. Jesus, I trust in You.

Tenth Station: Jesus Is Stripped of His Garments

The stripping of Your clothing reminds me of the excess baggage I carry to shield my true self from You and from others. I have not lived an authentic life. At times I masquerade as someone better—kinder, more agreeable, more humble, and less brusque—than I truly am. Your literal nakedness symbolizes my need for emotional and spiritual transparency. I, too, must be stripped of my barriers and distractions, the things that clutter my life and take over my heart. These are the idols I have made and sustained through my unrelenting façade. But here, now, I want to be exposed as you are—to be finally real, honest, and sincere. Take all that I am not, Jesus, so that I may be all that I am in You.

Eleventh Station: Jesus Is Nailed to the Cross

The nails are affixed to Your wrists with a jolting cadence, and with each blow, your face cringes in excruciating agony. You have not complained or uttered many words since this trial befell You in the garden, yet I gripe and grouse when I don't get my way or when my life gets harder to manage or bear. Suffering is not easy, and certainly You have exhibited this, but my call to relinquish the minor irritations and significant grievances into Your hands through these nails is evident now. I am the cause of Your Crucifixion, but You have presented me with an opportunity to change the course of my destiny. The nails that cause Your death are the same nails in my heart each time it breaks or experiences betrayal. When I give those nails back to You, I am changed through that suffering.

Twelfth Station: Jesus Dies on the Cross

Death has arrived, but not swiftly or mercifully. At times my life seems riddled with cruel and calloused circumstances, many beyond my control. Death is no stranger to me, and I know one day it will conquer and claim me among the wandering souls in Purgatory. But for now, I live while You perish. You have given me a second chance, Jesus, a chance to redirect the course of my life. Your death teaches me so much about myself—not merely about death alone, but also about living and what it means to thrive. I know that a sensory death must occur before this reawakening within my soul can fully flourish, but I am finally ready to embark on that road—my Calvary. Here I am, Lord. I come to do Your will.

Thirteenth Station: Jesus Is Taken Down from the Cross

Although Your body is removed from this gruesome scene, I still see You in my mind's eye. I will never forget such a sight, and today is the first day of my life that I have ever known what it means to grow in Your love—to become love as You have today. Your physical absence casts a pall over the hill, and many who cursed, spat, and scourged You are now weeping with remorse. Conversions are happening all around me because of Your great love, Jesus, and my heart is changing, too.

From Grief to Grace

Fourteenth Station: Jesus Is Laid in the Tomb
Your Passion and Death seemed to transpire in a frenzied flurry of activity, yet now You are in the tomb. Now is a period of waiting, expectant anticipation. For how long You are asking me to wait for the joy that comes in the morning remains a mystery to me. Still I wait with perseverance, with patience. Sometimes the waiting is part of my own cross, Jesus, because I do not know when the blessing of Resurrection will arrive. But I know it will, indeed, arrive according to Your perfect will and timing. My confidence in You grows, and I use this time of waiting to praise and thank You for teaching me how to love You and others through my suffering.

Reflection on the Resurrection
At last the fulfillment of Your promises has come. The tomb is empty, but Your presence still lingers there. As I enter, my heart flutters with earnest hope. Hope is the virtue that has gotten me this far, along with faith. I have learned the value of fidelity to You, especially during impossible and seemingly horrific times of my life. The tombs of darkness always produce the fruit of resurrection through perseverant waiting. Today death has been annihilated. I know that one day my own suffering will cease, and when it does, I will enter into that eternal ecstasy for which I have striven these long years.

Meditations

First Sorrowful Mystery: The Agony in the Garden
Jesus, I meet You in the garden, although I conceal my presence out of fear. Everything seems to be amiss, and my heart tells me that something is gravely wrong. I've never seen You so distraught, yet Your battle is clearly distressing You to the point of trembling and sweating blood. What can I do? I want to remain with You, but I am afraid—afraid that You might beckon me to join You, and I'm not ready for that yet. Instead, I wish to remain a bystander, although my heart is breaking. I long to comfort You, although I know that no consolation will suffice in this hour.

Second Sorrowful Mystery: The Scourging at the Pillar
The suffering is more visible and public now, a display of humiliation and carnage. Have I participated in Your scourging somehow, unbeknownst to me until this moment? Shame sweeps over me as I ponder this possibility. For a second, Your gaze meets mine, and our eyes lock in a wordless conversation. It is a conversation of two hearts that are wounded, although my affliction is warranted and Yours is unfounded. Somehow You are justifying mine through the horrors I witness, and the blood poured out from Your body is lessening the pain in mine. My heart leaps as I consider the hope of this day, despite the injustice.

Third Sorrowful Mystery: The Crowning with Thorns
Watching You mocked and scorned with a crown of thorns puncturing Your head is more than I can bear. Perhaps I was too hasty in concluding the hope I saw in Your glance. How I wish I could

wear the crown with You, Jesus. You are my love, my hope, but why must this happen? As I helplessly stand by Your side, my inability to rescue You from this senseless drama of agony cripples me. I am enraged, and yet Your pain quiets my spirit. I do not yet fully understand how suffering can yield such healing, but I trust You. I will walk with You to Calvary.

Fourth Sorrowful Mystery: Jesus Carries the Cross
The Cross appears intolerably weighty. In a brief instant, it occurs to me that You are upholding the onus of mankind. I am part of Your burden, so guilt creeps in as I begin to weep at this admittance of insult. Now Your injuries are truly my own, and my heart weeps as the tears cascade in a steady stream. The release of tension mystifies me as I watch the weight of the Cross nearly crush You. Still, my love for You is magnified as I bear this grief alongside You. Jesus, I am beginning to see that love cannot be separated from sacrifice. You are my love, and I long to love as You do.

Fifth Sorrowful Mystery: The Crucifixion and Death of Jesus
As Your body perishes in the heat of the day, I suddenly realize that my heart is parched. I, too, thirst, but for what? For salvation. Is this the moment of my redemption? Could it be that Your Crucifixion paves the way for my interior death? I slowly nod as a solitary tear trickles down my face. Your lifeless body hangs in the midafternoon breeze, and I am now forever changed. I cannot deny You the same love You have displayed today, but I perceive that this means nothing less than self-denial. I must freely, totally, faithfully, and fruitfully sacrifice all that I have and all that I am for Your sake, for the sake of love. If You permit me to suffer, I will do so with gratitude that I am

able to walk even more closely by Your side, understanding more comprehensively the depth of Your Passion. Your death is not the end, but the beginning of my journey to rediscovering love as You pave the way for continued healing in my life. Thank You, Jesus, my love and my all.

From Grief to Grace

THE SEVEN SORROWS OF MARY

The First Sorrow: The Prophecy
of Simeon (Luke 2:34–35)

As the sword pierces your heart, it lances mine, too. You have suffered the prophecy that bore your bittersweet mission: the hope for all humanity in your womb — our cause for rejoicing — will become a contradiction and suffer an unimaginable death. As the Mother of my Savior, you have become my mother in this moment, and I know that you suffer with me when I weep and am enshrouded in darkness.

Second Sorrow: The Flight into Egypt (Matthew 2:13–14)

How confounding to flee your native land into a foreign country, my Lady. Did you question what was happening or second-guess Joseph's leadership? No. Yet how often do I doubt God's guidance into unknown territory in my life? I marvel at your confidence, your unwavering trust in God, especially at a time of political upheaval and personal strife. I am reminded by your simplicity and humility that all of my life is truly an adventure, and I am cradled in the arms of Jesus and in your heart when I travel to unfamiliar and unwanted grief.

Third Sorrow: The Loss of the Child Jesus
in the Temple (Luke 2:43–45)

For a mother, there is no greater tragedy than losing a child: the panic and the agony of separation are unbearable. I consider the times in my life when I have gone astray from my Faith, especially when I have sinned or turned away from Jesus. In turning away from Him, I break your heart, too. How often have you relentlessly searched for me when I have been lost? In you, I have an eternal Mother whose warmth and kindness draws me back to where I belong — in Jesus' arms.

Fourth Sorrow: The Meeting of Jesus and Mary on the Way of the Cross

What happens at that intersection, in that brief moment when your heart and Jesus' bleeding heart unite? Yes, it is a lasting union of hearts, but this moment is a particularly brutal one. Jesus suffers both a mystical and literal Crucifixion, but yours is a white martyrdom. It always has been, but somehow in this meeting of hearts, your own passion intensifies. It is nearly complete, dear Mary. Our Mother, my Mother, know that my heart is with yours. My love for you grows exponentially as I long for you to know that you are not alone in this journey — and neither am I.

Fifth Sorrow: The Crucifixion

One cannot fathom a mother's agony at such an unspeakable act of violence upon her only son — the Son of God and Son of Man. Your abandonment, O Mary, is not yet complete, yet you continually capitulate to it as the horror finalizes with the death of God. Somehow you know death does not have the final say, although the rest of us wonder what will happen next. Your trust in the Father joins with your spousal union with the Holy Spirit. He carries you through this death, and I realize that you carry me through my own deaths: losing loved ones, dying to myself, moving, changing, and growing.

Sixth Sorrow: The Taking Down of the Body of Jesus from the Cross

O Mother of Sorrows, my tears mingle with yours today. Your maternal heart is beckoning me with a fountain of love, and my response has always been to run from this type of love. I've settled for incomplete and worldly gratifications, because I know that authentic love requires everything I have and am. Am I ready for this life of suffering? Perhaps, if I know you will share it with me. A child always needs a mother, and I must become that child—pure of heart, simple, trusting—so that you can lead me back to my Heavenly Father.

The Seventh Sorrow: The Burial of Jesus

The loss is too great, and I fear I can no longer bear the weight of such a heinous and hideous act. In my revulsion, I turn to you, and your gentle spirit strengthens me somehow. I don't know if I can believe as you do—that life has just begun and Jesus has truly conquered sin and death. I say that I believe, but logic deceives my faith. Yours is undaunted, and you quietly take my hand, guiding me to the tomb where I watch and wait for what is to come. I wait in silent anticipation. I do believe, Jesus. Help my unbelief.

Meditations

Prayer after Personal Meditation[52]

O my God, I give You heartfelt thanks for all the graces You have conferred on me during this meditation. Pardon me, I beseech You, for all the negligence and all the distractions of which I have been guilty. Give me strength to carry out the resolutions that I have made. Fortify me, that henceforth I may diligently practice this virtue (avoid this fault, or perform this action) to Your honor.

Help me to keep my good resolutions, O sweet Virgin Mary; and, my good angel, recall them to my memory, if I should ever forget or neglect them.

---

[52] "Prayer after Meditation," Catholic.org, accessed November 22, 2015, http://www.catholic.org/prayers/prayer.php?p=2059.

Appendix C

The Will To Live: A Commentary on End-of-Life Issues

A burning question in the minds of many Catholics today is a morally theological one: What is morally acceptable or unacceptable for those who are dying? Advance directives, living wills, proxies, and powers of attorneys all come to mind when one is considering options for oneself or possibly for a loved one.

To answer such questions, one must first be aware of the difference between moral obligation and moral option. Moral obligation is that which the Church informs us is necessary, such as providing water, medicine, and warmth to a person on life support. Moral option is up to the individual (provided he or she is lucid to make such decisions about preferences for dying), who discerns in good conscience what directives to accept or decline. An example of this would be someone who is offered cutting-edge treatment that has not yet been declared safe and may involve unforeseen risks but has shown impressive results to reduce a particular cancer. In this case, the individual could either accept or refuse this treatment, based on a personal moral decision, and either way would be acceptable according to Church teaching.[53]

All end-of-life decisions must be made in the context of a well-formed conscience and informed consent of the individual making such decisions. The person must possess significant knowledge and be living out of the gift of redemptive suffering before considering advance directives, for instance. For one who is not well catechized, suffering may appear meaningless and death the ultimate end to human existence. To another, a misinformed understanding of who God is may influence consideration of physician-assisted suicide (when a doctor helps a person kill himself) or euthanasia (either active or passive means of poisoning or otherwise killing a person with a particular substance without the person's help); to him or her, God may be more of a distant figure who is indifferent toward our personal decisions (deism). Both beliefs are errant and warrant reconsideration.

For Catholics, advance directives should be clearly stated not to include physician-assisted suicide or euthanasia as an option if one is ill prepared to make such decisions when dying. Choosing a power of attorney (POA) or proxy is a grave matter, and the person should contemplate selecting someone who exhibits exceptional moral character and judgment, because the POA will make end-of-life decisions on behalf of the dying person. Some Catholics have opted out of a legally binding living will in favor of the alternative will to live.[54] Those in favor of such

[53] Based on "A Catholic Guide to End-of-Life Decisions," National Catholic Bioethics Center, accessed November 22, 2015, http://www.ncbcenter.org/page.aspx?pid=1204.
[54] "Will to Live, NOT Living Will," Priests for Life, accessed November 22, 2015, http://www.priestsforlife.org/euthanasia/livingwill.htm.

A Commentary on End-of-Life Issues

an option declare that living wills nebulously define "medication" and "artificial means," which may become nefariously used
legally to terminate one's life prematurely. Instead, the will to
live is a legal alternative that is soundly Catholic and assists the
individual in selecting a proxy for health-care decisions.
The United States Conference of Catholic Bishops provides
an incredible abundance of resources for the person pursuing
more specific information on pain management, suicide, and
euthanasia,[55] which present a comprehensive understanding
of potential moral predicaments that are not clearly defined
through the basic understanding of morally acceptable end-of-
life directives.

In the secular mindset, "death with dignity" has become a
euphemism for compassionate means to taking one's life—and
death—into one's own hands. Instead of "life with dignity," post-
modernists believe that "quality of life," should determine who
lives and for how long. This suggests that some lives are worth
more than others and that, when one's "quality of life" deterio-
rates to a subjective measure, then assisted-suicide or euthanasia
is a viable option to living with suffering. As Catholics, we know
that all humans have a right to live; thus, we should also "will
to live" so as to fulfill God's command to "choose life, that you
and your descendants may live" (Deut. 30:19).

---

[55] For more information, visit http://www.usccb.org/issues-and-
action/human-life-and-dignity/end-of-life/.

203

Bibliography

Ahern, Patrick. *Three Gifts of Thérèse of Lisieux: A Saint for Our Times*. New York: Crown, 2014.

American Psychiatric Association. *Diagnostic and Statistical Manual of Mental Disorders*. 5th ed. Washington, DC: American Psychiatric Association, 2013.

Da Bergamo, Cajetan Mary. *Humility of Heart*. 3rd ed. Charlotte, NC: TAN Books, 2006.

D'Elbée, Jean C. J. *I Believe in Love: A Personal Retreat Based on the Teaching of St. Thérèse of Lisieux*. Manchester, NH: Sophia Institute Press, 2001.

De Caussade, Jean-Pierre. *Abandonment to Divine Providence*. New York: Doubleday Dell, 1975.

St. Ignatius of Loyola. *The Spiritual Exercises of Saint Ignatius*. New York: Doubleday Dell, 1989.

St. John of the Cross. *The Collected Works of St. John of the Cross*. Washington, DC: Institute of Carmelite Studies, 1979.

Kübler-Ross, Elisabeth. *On Death and Dying: What the Dying Have to Teach Doctors, Nurses, Clergy, and Their Own Families*. New York, New York: Scribner, 2014.

Kushner, Harold. S. *When Bad Things Happen to Good People.* New York: Anchor, 2004.

O'Dell, Catherine. *Father Solanus: The Story of Solanus Casey, O.F.M. Cap.* 2nd ed. Huntington, IN: Our Sunday Visitor, 1995.

About the Author

Jeannie Ewing

Jeannie Ewing believes the world focuses too much on superficial happiness and then crumbles when sorrow strikes. Because life is about more than what makes us feel fuzzy inside, she writes about the hidden value of suffering and even discovering joy in the midst of grief. Jeannie shares her heart as a mom of two girls with special needs in *Navigating Deep Waters: Meditations for Caregivers.* She was featured on National Public Radio's *Weekend Edition* and dozens of other radio shows and podcasts. For more information, please visit her websites lovealonecreates.com and fromgrief2grace.com. You can also find Jeannie on Facebook and Twitter. Please use hashtag #fromgrief2grace when conversing about the book on social media.

Sophia Institute

Sophia Institute is a nonprofit institution that seeks to nurture the spiritual, moral, and cultural life of souls and to spread the Gospel of Christ in conformity with the authentic teachings of the Roman Catholic Church.

Sophia Institute Press fulfills this mission by offering translations, reprints, and new publications that afford readers a rich source of the enduring wisdom of mankind.

Sophia Institute also operates two popular online Catholic resources: CrisisMagazine.com and CatholicExchange.com.

Crisis Magazine provides insightful cultural analysis that arms readers with the arguments necessary for navigating the ideological and theological minefields of the day. *Catholic Exchange* provides world news from a Catholic perspective as well as daily devotionals and articles that will help you to grow in holiness and live a life consistent with the teachings of the Church.

In 2013, Sophia Institute launched Sophia Institute for Teachers to renew and rebuild Catholic culture through service to Catholic education. With the goal of nurturing the spiritual, moral, and cultural life of souls, and an abiding respect for the role and work of teachers, we strive to provide materials and programs that are at once enlightening to the mind and ennobling to the heart; faithful and complete, as well as useful and practical.

Sophia Institute gratefully recognizes the Solidarity Association for preserving and encouraging the growth of our apostolate over the course of many years. Without their generous and timely support, this book would not be in your hands.

www.SophiaInstitute.com
www.CatholicExchange.com
www.CrisisMagazine.com
www.SophiaInstituteforTeachers.org

Sophia Institute Press® is a registered trademark of Sophia Institute.
Sophia Institute is a tax-exempt institution as defined by the
Internal Revenue Code, Section 501(c)(3). Tax I.D. 22-2548708.